# A Field Guide to Ghost Guns

# A Field Guide to Ghost Guns

## For Police and Forensic Investigations

Robert E. Walker

CRC Press is an imprint of the
Taylor & Francis Group, an **informa** business

First edition published 2022
by CRC Press
6000 Broken Sound Parkway NW, Suite 300, Boca Raton, FL 33487-2742

and by CRC Press
2 Park Square, Milton Park, Abingdon, Oxon, OX14 4RN

© 2022 Taylor & Francis Group, LLC
CRC Press is an imprint of Taylor & Francis Group, LLC

Reasonable efforts have been made to publish reliable data and information, but the author and publisher cannot assume responsibility for the validity of all materials or the consequences of their use. The authors and publishers have attempted to trace the copyright holders of all material reproduced in this publication and apologize to copyright holders if permission to publish in this form has not been obtained. If any copyright material has not been acknowledged please write and let us know so we may rectify in any future reprint.

Except as permitted under U.S. Copyright Law, no part of this book may be reprinted, reproduced, transmitted, or utilized in any form by any electronic, mechanical, or other means, now known or hereafter invented, including photocopying, microfilming, and recording, or in any information storage or retrieval system, without written permission from the publishers.

For permission to photocopy or use material electronically from this work, access www.copyright.com or contact the Copyright Clearance Center, Inc. (CCC), 222 Rosewood Drive, Danvers, MA 01923, 978-750-8400. For works that are not available on CCC please contact mpkbookspermissions@tandf.co.uk

*Trademark notice*: Product or corporate names may be trademarks or registered trademarks and are used only for identification and explanation without intent to infringe.

*Library of Congress Cataloging-in-Publication Data*
Names: Walker, Robert E., 1973- author.
Title: A field guide to ghost guns : for police and forensic investigations / Robert E. Walker.
Identifiers: LCCN 2021023015 (print) | LCCN 2021023016 (ebook) | ISBN 9780367490959 (hbk) | ISBN 9781032125305 (pbk) | ISBN 9781003044499 (ebk)
Subjects: LCSH: Home-built firearms. | Firearms and crime.
Classification: LCC TS535 .W24 2022 (print) | LCC TS535 (ebook) | DDC 364.2--dc23
LC record available at https://lccn.loc.gov/2021023015
LC ebook record available at https://lccn.loc.gov/2021023016

ISBN: 978-0-367-49095-9 (hbk)
ISBN: 978-1-032-12530-5 (pbk)
ISBN: 978-1-003-04449-9 (ebk)

DOI: 10.4324/9781003044499

Typeset in Minion
by Deanta Global Publishing Services, Chennai, India

*This work is dedicated to my lovely wife, Jayne, and our three children, Sam, Ava, and Max, who are all partners in this craft. Congratulations, we did it again.*

# Contents

| | |
|---|---|
| Acknowledgments | xi |
| Foreword | xiii |
| Preface | xv |
| About the Author | xix |

**1 A Brief History of Gun Making**     1

| | |
|---|---|
| The Self-Made Gun Movement | 5 |
| The Ghost Gun | 6 |
| Improvised Firearms Are Not Ghost Guns | 10 |
| The Role of Technology in the Ghost Gun Debate | 12 |
| The Do-It-Yourself Culture | 15 |
| The "Prepper" Movement | 17 |
| Political Motivations | 18 |
| The Privately Made Firearm and the Criminal Enterprise | 19 |
| Brain Trust: Potential Benefits of Self-Manufactured Firearms | 20 |
| Notes | 21 |
| References | 23 |

**2 Regulated and Non-Regulated Manufacturing**     25

| | |
|---|---|
| Regulated and Non-Regulated Firearm Manufacturing Activity | 25 |
| Regulated Firearms Manufacturing Activity in the United States | 29 |
| Growth Trend in Licensed Manufacturers | 30 |
| 2020 into 2021 Firearm Sales Trends | 31 |
| Opposition to Non-Regulated Manufacturing | 32 |
| Legalities Affecting the Final Configuration of Self-Made Firearms | 34 |
| Firearm Types and Definitions | 35 |
| Self-Manufacture of a Regulated Firearm | 40 |
| Notes | 42 |
| References | 45 |

**3 The Frame, Firearm Components, and Firearm Accessories**     47

| | |
|---|---|
| Crossing the Threshold: Is It a Receiver or a Blank? | 47 |

| | | |
|---|---|---|
| | Functional versus Operable | 51 |
| | Safety Considerations | 54 |
| | Non-Guns | 54 |
| | Components, Parts, and Accessories | 57 |
| | Non-Regulated Components | 58 |
| | Serial Numbered Parts | 61 |
| | Notes | 62 |
| | References | 62 |
| **4** | **Fabricating a Receiver and Assembling a Firearm** | **63** |
| | Additive Manufacturing and 3D Printing | 63 |
| | Tools, Jigs, and Fixtures | 67 |
| | CNC Machinery | 72 |
| | Variations in Receiver Materials | 74 |
| |     Machine Steel Receivers | 74 |
| |     Polymer | 74 |
| |     Metal Injection Molding | 75 |
| |     Cast or Forged Receivers | 75 |
| | Assembling and Finishing the Self-Made Receiver | 75 |
| | Notes | 77 |
| | References | 78 |
| **5** | **Common Types of Ghost Guns** | **79** |
| | The Armalite Pattern | 79 |
| | The Model 1911 and Variants | 85 |
| | Glock Pattern Handguns | 87 |
| | Ruger 10/22 | 89 |
| | The AK-Type Firearm | 90 |
| | The Liberator | 91 |
| | Tubular Receiver Firearms | 92 |
| | Suppressors | 92 |
| | Original Designs and Hybrid Patterns | 94 |
| | Notes | 96 |
| | Reference | 96 |
| **6** | **Investigative Considerations** | **97** |
| | Investigative Methods and Techniques for Interdicting Contraband Arms | 98 |
| |     Traffic Stops | 98 |
| |     Controlled Buys | 99 |
| | Controlled Delivery | 101 |

| | |
|---|---|
| Can a Criminal Manufacture a Firearm? | 102 |
| Lost or Stolen Firearms | 102 |
| Straw Sales | 104 |
| Theft | 105 |
| Multi-Jurisdictional Co-Responsibility and Task Forces | 105 |
| Firearm Tracing | 106 |
| Firearm Safety and Evidentiary Concerns | 110 |
| Investigative Circumstances | 111 |
| Encounters with Suspected Privately Made Firearms | 112 |
| Potential Evidence | 113 |
| National Integrated Ballistics Information Network (NIBIN) | 114 |
| Dealing with Persons | 115 |
| Digital Forensics | 116 |
| Coordination with Prosecutors | 117 |
| Notes | 118 |
| References | 118 |

# Index  121

# Acknowledgments

*Over the course of our lives, many of us have the good fortune of encountering others who play a pivotal role in our lives – they enlighten, inspire, and cultivate the habits of the mind. We are influenced in many ways by others who serve to set an example of what to do or not to do, and I have been acquainted with both. There are many to whom I owe a debt of gratitude for helping me to get where I am. I cannot name all of you here at the risk of carelessly overlooking someone, but you will know who you are, and I deeply appreciate your council, mentorship, and wisdom.*

*A special thank you to the folks at Defense Distributed for the images of the Ghost Gunner 3 that appear in this text.*

*And finally, I want once again to extend my special thanks to those of you who, in your own way, continue to inspire me to put my thoughts into words and words to paper, which brings forth this text.*

# Foreword

From the first chapter of *A Field Guide to Ghost Guns: For Police and Forensic Investigations*, where the history of gun manufacturing provides a nostalgic look back to the Golden Age of engineering and manufacturing of firearms – much of which was borne out of a necessity to preserve life, freedom, and the democratic ideals of Western civilization – this book informs the reader how the past has shaped the present in the manufacture of firearms. The rise in the homemade manufacture of firearms, or so-called "ghost guns," coincides with the rise of the internet and fear of a growing surveillance state. This perceived threat, real or otherwise, stems from an ever-growing and intrusive government that seeks more and more control over the lives of its citizens. As the surveillance state grows through the collection of metadata, those with the means and the know-how are themselves taking advantage of technology to manufacture firearms outside of the boundaries and limitations of the Gun Control Act. While some would say that these citizen gunmakers are exploiting loopholes in the Act, others would simply state that these resourceful individuals are just using their rights guaranteed under the U.S. Constitution.

The number of these resourceful citizens will likely only grow larger and more determined. After the governmental lockdowns of the Covid-19 pandemic, which imposed severe restrictions on people's civil liberties and freedom of movement, the suspicion and fear of government has increased. Moreover, the nationwide civil unrest of 2020 caused many to fear for their physical safety. As a result, record numbers of citizens are purchasing firearms at rates so high that gun stores are having problems keeping their stores stocked with inventory. When you combine the current public atmosphere and the heavy demand for firearms with a perceived governmental ideology that seeks to limit firearms ownership, the number of homemade firearms not subject to governmental registration is only bound to increase in the future.

Thus, the term "ghost guns" will almost certainly become a familiar and often used phrase in the public discourse. *A Field Guide to Ghost Guns: For Police and Forensic Investigations* is a necessary read for anyone who wants to educate themselves about how and why "ghost guns" are manufactured. Although "assault weapons" is the term used for the moment in today's political debate about firearms restrictions, "ghost guns" will be the term used for the political debate of tomorrow and the foreseeable future. *A Field Guide* to *Ghost Guns: For Police and Forensic Investigations* is the first book that imparts a level of knowledge to the reader that previously was only known to certain members of law enforcement with expertise in firearms, such as the BATF and the FBI.

  **–Jean-Paul Galasso**, *Esq., B.C.S., Board Certified Criminal Trial Attorney*

# Preface

Firearms are a divisive subject, one that there seems to be little, if any, common ground remaining in American political discourse. The individual's and the collective's access to and ownership of firearms is articulated in the Second Amendment of the United States Constitution, "A well-regulated Militia, being necessary to the security of a free State, the right of the people to keep and bear Arms shall not be infringed." The pedant among us relishes the dissection of the exact meanings hidden within the combination, order, scope, and original intent of the words in this verbiage, which has evolved into a debate defined more by the minutia and semantics than the basic premise. The disputation is far down the rabbit hole in pursuit of subtleties: barrel lengths, how the ammunition storage mechanism is attached to the firearm, the style of stock, to name a few. All of these essentially "nibble around the edges," establishing public policy by way of *incrementalism* while avoiding the core issue altogether. Some 90 years of enacting laws and effectuating regulation by this incrementalism has resulted in a bizarre mishmash of laws at the local, state, and federal levels. Firearms and ammunition legal to make, sell, and possess in certain venues are prohibited in others. Some firearms only remain legal as they were graciously granted a *grandfather* alibi, that is they were made before a certain date, after which further manufacture or importation was prohibited. Consider the term "assault weapon," two words joined together in an effort to identify this or that firearm by the presence of some chosen characteristics or mere appearances, but absent any objective consideration to the actual function, which, incidentally, is already regulated.

The debate over firearms in the United States is portrayed stereotypically as an issue drawn straight down the political lines, one said to clearly separate the right from the left, but this is an intellectually lazy, if not blatantly dishonest, presentation of the facts. Conventional wisdom has the rhetoric of the right tending to wholly support gun rights, whereas the left tends to favor less accessibility, greater restrictions, and perhaps even an outright prohibition on private gun ownership, but this dogma is, at best, a half-truth. Here is an undisputable, non-partisan fact: in the past 50 years, there have been four major federal initiatives curtailing accessibility to firearms: two were enacted by supposedly gun-favoring Republican presidents, and the other two by Democrat presidents, who at least partially achieved their political ambitions. This does not seem to support a theory of an alleged deep political divide, for if this were so, at least two of these initiatives would not exist, at least as they played out. Regardless, the end result was the same: incrementalism leaves both sides claiming defeat – either the new laws went too far in their reach to create an infringement of rights, or they did not go far enough. Look at the 1968 Gun Control Act for an example, which has been amended numerous times as it did not seem to go far enough. Even as this book prepares to go to press, further regulatory measures are sought which will amend meanings as prescribed in the act itself. Meanwhile, courtrooms are filled with lawsuits emanating from all varieties of plaintiffs – government entities and subdivisions, well-funded special interests, and even an occasionally named individual. If we cannot affect policy change through political processes, we can just force the question through litigation and regulatory newspeak. These new proposals will be litigated too, leaving in limbo the public and surviving exemplars of the articles in controversy.

Innumerable candidates seeking all levels of elected office have campaigned uttering the platitudes of "sensible" or "common sense" gun control, setting up the false argument using equivocation to complete the deception. Ironically, in more recent times, the veiled political double-talk and abstruse language has fallen away, somewhat refreshingly. For contrast, not too many campaign seasons ago there was an obviously staged photo op showing a candidate carrying a shotgun while emerging from an early morning hunt. The event was so shamelessly glib it came off as absurd at the least; an attempt at *argumentum ad populum*. Somehow the voting sportsman, the hunter, would be more at ease with a shotgun totting candidate while those less inclined to gun rights would not be offended by such a bona fide display of, well, a sportsman. But this style of non-committal political posturing is losing its effectiveness to sway the voter. More recently, within a gaggle of candidates, at least one made their intentions very clear, promising to promptly and aggressively confiscate firearms from private hands if elected.

In the rest of the world, gun laws are found on the extreme ends of the spectrum, ranging from non-existent all the way to outright prohibition and every shade of variation in between. In countries where there is at least passageway to privileged ownership, this in no way guarantees any such requests will ever be heard or honored. Privileges granted by a government are easily denied or withdrawn. Many nations allow citizens to maintain their own arms. The antithesis of gun control was Switzerland, where, until relatively recently, law required all homes to possess firearms, but this has gradually evolved with internal and European pressure.

Law and regulation are an industry in and unto itself. As long as a society will pay for people to regulate for a living, there will always be regulations. As long as there are lawmakers who think, maybe even truly believe, that writing a new law will actually have an impact on curbing behaviors, a stream

# Preface xvii

of bills passed to the executive to sign will follow. These laws may well punish convicted offenders, but laws have never proven to be an effective crime deterrent. In my own experience in casework, I never knew a time when persons engaging in criminal conduct have concerned themselves with breaking the law, only in how best to avoid detection and identification; and when apprehended how to best strategize getting out from underneath the charges without ever directly addressing the basic question- did you do it? There are numerous real-world cases cited in this book, and nearly all of them involved parties who were either prohibited from possessing a firearm – whether it is a ghost gun; an arm made by a licensed, professional manufacturer; or an illegally manufactured firearm. In an era when it is said there are calls for "criminal justice reforms" aimed at policing, reduced or eliminated bail, decriminalizing recreational drugs, and rethinking sentencing and incarceration, it is ironic that there would be any serious consideration paid to creating more gun law; as existing laws go unenforced there is drive to make more laws.

This book is focused on the technical aspects of self-made firearms; however, the topic does not exist in a bubble. It boils over into the broader gun rights question, free speech, and the competing interests of governmental oversight and individual liberties. Laws are necessary to maintain a peaceful and orderly society, but there are activities that fall outside the rationale for law in the first place – a government, acting on behalf of society, has a compelling interest to restrict or regulate an activity. Historically, laws have addressed the fundamental natural laws – theft, rape, murder – but now there is a fixation on excessively specific definitions of the natural laws – a theft is theft, for example, whether it entails shoplifting or using a stolen credit card for online purchases; in fact, each is still a theft. We have all heard stories or seen articles ridiculing laws on the books somewhere that seem archaic or even downright absurd. Whatever it was, it must have seemed a worthy cause at the time, however impetuous it was.

The purpose of this text is to educate and inform readers about the self-made firearm, the so-called ghost gun. In this text, you will see how the intersection of technology and scalable manufacturing have enabled individuals to undertake building their own firearms. This book is not intended to debate the baseline question of gun rights versus gun control or to try to square off interpretations of positive versus negative rights. The legal discussion within the text is merely provided for context and background. What matters is the thinking person has the intellectual honesty and integrity to approach a topic with a truly open mind and not to be blinded by preconceived notions. This attitude of objectivity and reason is an absolute necessity in the service of the public in the field of law enforcement. The professional investigator and the allied disciplines must always set aside their personal opinions in the interest of upholding the fair and just law. A properly credentialled and competent examiner renders an opinion, predicated on their observations of the evidence offered and made in a fair and impartial spirit with the utmost integrity. If no violation occurred, then let it be so.

**Robert Walker**
*August 2021*

# About the Author

**Robert Walker** began working in the field of crime scene investigation in 1995. In 1996, he entered an apprenticeship under the tutelage of a noted firearm expert and first qualified to render expert testimony in a court of law on a firearm case in 1999.

In 2010, Walker earned his Certified Crime Scene Investigator rating through the International Association for Identification. He qualified as an expert under both Frye and Daubert standards in firearms, among other subjects, in the state of Florida's Twentieth Judicial Circuit, the Federal Middle District of Florida, and the Federal Western District of Texas. Walker was an active teacher, serving as an adjunct faculty member at several colleges and a police academy instructor. Walker remains active as a firearms instructor and lecturer on topics related to crime scene investigation and firearms.

Walker is a graduate of Barry University in Miami Shores, Florida. During his career, he had the opportunity to attend training at the FBI Academy in Quantico, Virginia, the Office of the Chief Medical Examiner in New York City, and at the Miami-Dade Police Department. He is the author of *Cartridges and Firearm Identification* and *Crime Scene Basics and Beyond*.

# A Brief History of Gun Making

Gun making was once an artisan's craft. The maker was a blacksmith, tinkerer, engineer, and inventor. By designing, fabricating, and fitting parts, the gunmaker brought the three requisite elements together to fashion a functional firearm: a breech to hold a projectile and powder charge, an ignition system to detonate the powder charge, and a barrel from which to expel the projectile. The shooter would provide the impetus to initiate the action by pressing the trigger, which, in turn, set into motion a "firing train," the mechanical linkage joining the trigger to the ignition system. The breech and barrel in form and function were long settled, but the ignition system was subject to continuous evolution. Thus, numerous systems were devised – matchlock, wheellock, snaphaunce, flintlock, the percussion cap, and, ultimately, self-contained ammunition cartridges. One may have heard the idiom *lock, stock, and barrel*, meaning *the whole* or *everything*. This figure of speech has its origins in gun making; customers would take delivery of the completed firearm instead of purchasing just the barreled action (the "lock" and "barrel") from the gunmaker and obtaining the "stock" from another source or fashioning it themselves.

The real impediment in the evolution of firearm designs fell on the means by which the arms were loaded. The development of effective self-contained ammunition cartridges thrust small arms designs forward from muzzle loaders into all forms of repeaters. There was more evolution in small arms from 1865 to 1905 then in the preceding 200 years.

Industrialized gunmakers emerged in different parts of the world prior to and during the era called the "Industrial Revolution." The Italian firm Beretta, perhaps one of the oldest standing trademarks in the world, claims it originated in 1526. In what was once known as the Kingdom of Prussia, now modern-day Germany, gunmaker J.P. Sauer & Sohn was established in 1751 and remains in business today. The middle nineteenth century saw the emergence of many of the names that became synonymous with gun manufacturing – from the United States, Colt in 1836, Remington in 1839, and Winchester in 1866. In 1889, a consortium of gun makers joined together to form Fabrique Nationale in Herstal, Belgium. As time went on, arms manufacturers fell into the sphere of two different structures – privately held and operated businesses or state-controlled operations. The existence of one or the other is often determined by the political sphere where it is located[1] and by the practical necessities of a national defense industrial base. As industrialization became the standard by which goods were made, the assembly-line worker replaced the artisan, and gun making passed from the hands of the craftsman into the hands of the factory worker – assembler, machinist, fitter, finisher, and so forth. Arms manufacturing was a natural fit for the principles of mass production: standardized pattern firearms were faster and cheaper to produce and interchangeable parts allowed firearms to be repaired or refurbished with ease. The Industrial Revolution begat improved materials and new metal working processes, machine tools, and approaches to fabricating components. Governments ordered many thousands of firearms in peacetime and countless more during times of war. Standardized firearm patterns greatly simplified the army's logistics: common ammunition, accoutrements, and training. Furthermore, practically any manufacturer could be engaged in manufacturing arms insomuch as suitable tooling was available and the patterns and plans were supplied. Figure 1.1 depicts a modern reproduction of the U.S. Army's Model 1873 Trapdoor Carbine.[2] The arm was originally manufactured by the U.S. Arsenal at Springfield, Massachusetts, and was designed for the U.S. Army from the outset. The 1873 was produced in keeping with the gun making paradigm of the day – wooden stock and finished quality grade steel. The 1873 was made both as a full-length infantry arm and the handier carbine version was intended for cavalry troops.

During the Second World War, the paradigm of gun manufacturing made a significant shift. The firearms that armed the combatants at the start of the conflict had, for the most part, changed little from the First World War; however, such was the scale of conflict, the demand for small arms stressed the industrial might of all the belligerent nations.[3] Figure 1.2 shows an American defense worker using a machine tool to produce parts for 1911A1 pistols. It appears she is employed by Colt from the badge worn on the overalls.

Early in the conflict, many arms were manufactured using most, if not all, machined parts, but, by war's end, firearm designs had changed

**Figure 1.1** A modern reproduction of the U.S. Army's Model 1873 Springfield Trapdoor Carbine. This pattern arm was carried into action by the doomed U.S. Army's 7th Cavalry at the Little Big Horn (Image courtesy of Uberti).

# A Brief History of Gun Making

**Figure 1.2** Anna Healey turns and drills butt millings on the ejector of .45-caliber automatic pistols in the plant of a large manufacturer of firearms. This plant produced pistols, machine guns, and other weapons that would soon be spreading trouble for the Axis. Many men and women were employed here producing pistols, machine guns, and other essential weapons for the armed forces (Image by Andreas Feininger; courtesy of Library of Congress).

dramatically, moving away from guns made of all machined steel parts and wooden stocks to parts and receivers fashioned from stamped and riveted sheet metal, forgings, castings, and even some use of plastics. Bakelite and Durofol are but two examples, introduced by Germany as a substitute material from which various grips and other gun furniture was fashioned. Shortages of skilled labor, manufacturing expediency, cost, and conservation of strategic materials were all factors; let alone changes in battlefield tactics, which ushered in a new generation of small arms. Consider the pistol slide depicted in Figure 1.3; just to fabricate this single piece required a considerable number of milling operations that required time, machinery,

**Figure 1.3** World War Two era P.38 pistol slide. Shaped from a single block of steel, the machining marks are evident. At this stage of the conflict, production numbers were prioritized over polish and finish. The stamped characters are the serial number, the code 'ac' to mask the manufacturer's identity, and the year "44" (Image from author's collection).

high grade material, and skilled labor, all of which are precious commodities in a wartime situation.

In the post-war era, arms manufacturing methods, practices, and technology evolved rapidly, especially in materials science and machine tools. By the 1950s, alternatives to machine grade steel and wood were not only contemplated but were in use. The Armalite Corporation,[4] a subsidiary of Fairchild Aircraft, developed a series of firearms, calling them "AR" for "Armalite Rifle," among them were the AR-10 and the AR-15.[5] Armalite was formed with the intention of conceiving the next generation of small arms, using aerospace materials and radically different approach to firearm design. In the AR-10 and AR-15 rifle concepts, Armalite opted to use an aluminum forging for the receiver – lightweight, impervious to the elements, and strong. Armalite was not alone in its endeavors to explore alternative materials. The Nylon 66, a creation of the Remington Arms Company, was a rifle constructed of material of the same name, proving that not only were composite materials a viable option, but it also actually offered advantages over wood and metal. A traditional wooden gunstock would warp, flex, and eventually deteriorate if exposed to wet environments and humidity, but none of these would affect a polymer. Now, in the twenty-first century, it is the norm to use materials other than steel and wood to manufacture firearms, firearm components, and accessories. Glock is one of the best-selling handgun brands in the world. Initially met with scoffs from the industry and outright falsehoods at its introduction, the Glock overcame the initial skepticisms, and, in fact, its success not only forced its competitors to take a second look at the idea, but it also normalized polymer-framed handguns, making it an industry standard. Figure 1.4 shows one of Glock's many handgun models.

# A Brief History of Gun Making

**Figure 1.4** The Glock was not the first polymer-framed pistol, but it ushered in a whole new way of thinking about handgun design and materials. The shown example is the model 30 chambered in .45 ACP (Image from author's collection).

## The Self-Made Gun Movement

The interest in self-made firearms did not occur in a vacuum and coincides with other movements within the United States' firearms industry at large. Since 2004,[6] the industry has changed substantially with a great deal of creative effort invested in creating new styles of products compliant with applicable law and regulation while, at the same time, finding workarounds within the language of those same laws. Many of these products are not new designs but are existing firearm patterns merely reimagined and reinvigorated into new configurations. Consider what has become known as the *large-format handgun*. Such a handgun may use a "pistol stabilizing brace"[7] in lieu of a different style grip and is in direct contrast to a rifle version of a similar firearm, which would have a shoulder stock. Large-format handguns, even absent such a brace, are criticized as merely a thinly veiled effort to circumvent registration requirements for manufacturing or possessing a short-barreled rifle; however, a firearm categorized as a handgun[8] is just that – a handgun – regardless of its appearance, to speak nothing of its function, which is unchanged no matter the aesthetics or the type of configuration. Figure 1.5 depicts a large-format handgun, as the model is offered for sale by the manufacturer.

Likewise, models such as the Mossberg Shockwave,[9] as shown in Figure 1.6, are legally defined as a *firearm* but do not meet the legal definitions

**Figure 1.5** Ruger AR-556 pistol chambered in .350 Legend. Note the pistol stabilizing brace installed. This model illustrates the so-called *large-format handgun* (Image courtesy of Sturm, Ruger, & Co., Inc.).

**Figure 1.6** The Mossberg 590 Nightstick. This firearm would fool many into thinking it is a "sawn off shotgun" but, in fact, is a legally configured firearm and is sold in this configuration through ordinary retail outlets (Image courtesy of O.F. Mossberg & Sons, Inc.).

prescribed for a shotgun, handgun, or rifle, so they are simply categorized as *other*. Franklin Armory markets a firearm named the Reformation, which, by nature of its unique straight line bore profile (no spiral rifling or smooth bore), also falls into the gaps of the verbiage of federal laws.[10] While the Reformation may appear to be a short-barreled rifle, in fact, it is not because of this unique barrel design feature.

## The Ghost Gun

> *This right here has the ability with a .30-caliber clip to disperse with 30 bullets within half a second. Thirty magazine clip in half a second.*
>
> *–Kevin de Leon, a California state senator*

A California senator uttered these remarks at a press conference in 2014. The apparent intent was an attempt to call attention to homemade firearms or what became termed as *ghost guns*. This statement was riddled with factual and technical inaccuracies:

# A Brief History of Gun Making

- The terms .30 caliber and clip, as used here, create a solecism, as there is no correlation between a firearm's *caliber*[11] and a firearm's *clip*.[12]
- The presented firearm is incapable of "dispersing" (firing) "30 bullets within half a second." This would suggest the firearm has a rate of fire about 3,600 rounds per minute. This rate of fire is achieved by a relatively small number of multi-barreled Gatling-style firearms used by the armed forces.[13]
- The "thirty magazine clip" is another solecism, consisting of a series of disjointed terms that has no cohesive meaning.

The speaker argues for the urgent need to address the ghost gun through regulatory edict or legislative action. Never mind the fact this information seemed to be a series of talking points that were somehow confused between memorization and delivery. Thus, the term ghost gun was originally intended as a pejorative used to describe a firearm whose existence is known only by the one who crafted it. The connotation meant to insinuate imminent danger to a safe and orderly society. Speaking more precisely, a ghost gun is a homemade firearm, and its creation is not reported, nor is it recorded to any entity outside of whomever the builder confides. Like many pejoratives, it was embraced as a badge of honor and has since become a part of the lexicon. The term has gained such widespread acceptance that it now appears in laws and is part of common speech and its ordinary meaning apparently well understood.

The term ghost gun appeared in publication as early as October 2014 when writer Chandra Steele published an article in *PCMag.com* that profiled the work of Cody Wilson, founder of Defense Distributed, a company that was blending the Information Age and technology with homemade gun making. On its website, Defense Distributed claims it was started in 2012. "In 2012 Cody Wilson recruited a team to develop the first entirely three-dimensionally (3D) printed pistol, eventually named The Liberator" (Defense Distributed, n.d.). Another company involved in the homemade firearm industry, Stealth Arms, reports going into business in 2012, as well. "We started small, selling specialized targets from a modest workshop. But it didn't take long before we began designing our own custom 1911 frame and launching our flagship products, 80% Lowers in AR and 1911 formats" (Stealth Arms, n.d.). 80% Arms, a California-based company that sells supplies to home builders, states that it went into business in 2013. In an article published June 3, 2015, in *Wired* titled "I Made an Untraceable AR-15 'Ghost Gun' in my Office – and It Was Easy," writer Andy Greenberg recounted his own experience fabricating AR-15 lower receivers using three different methods – the Ghost Gunner CNC machine, using a drill press, and by 3D printing. After the experiment was finished, Greenberg surrendered all three lower receivers to police (Greenberg, 2015).

To fully understand the ghost gun, one must look at the evolution of the firearm-interest culture in contemporary times. Access to and private ownership of firearms by the private American citizen and the correlation[14] that has been drawn between firearms and crime has created a very complex and often convoluted legal patchwork. Most firearms laws have focused on manufacturers or manufacturing activity and not on the owner, ensuring that, no matter what the law or regulation was, no one could argue there was a de facto ban per se, but there could be restrictions imposed that could have the net effect of limiting choices and options in the marketplace.

The establishment view of firearms held that there were the big brand name gun makers, and one bought a catalog product. There were smaller name makers, but these were niche items and generally outside the interest and price range of the average customer. In either case there was little interest in privately making one's own firearm, and it likely was looked upon as one of several taboo topics within the firearms-interested community, notwithstanding the general misconceptions of the public concerning firearms. Even today, there are many people who believe there are absolute prohibitions against private ownership of machine guns and silencers,[15] which is not true. The author has heard many fallacies and myths passed about that supported this notion. It was almost as though there was a "social stratum" within the firearms community, to own a National Firearms Act regulated firearm was viewed as an elite opportunity, not something for just anyone, and almost had the aura of a club that not everyone was entitled to join and may have even been discouraged from attempting. In much the same vein, the subject of homemade firearms is all but an open secret, a topic that, until relatively recently, was almost as equally shrouded in mystery and misinformation. Perhaps, even passively, there were numerous factors that strategically worked to keep it that way.

- Lack of access to the law.
- The practice was never publicly advertised nor clarified to its legality.
- No readily accessible source from which to seek competent, credible counsel and guidance.
- A real or feigned distrust of a perceived anti-gun government intent on restricting access to firearms and aggressive prosecutions for an ever-growing list of firearm offenses.
- Allowing misinformation to pass along unchallenged.
- Obscuring the meaning of law in legalese and jargon, such that the average person could not or would not bother to try to understand it.

The mindset paralleled the Medieval view of world geography: the Earth was flat and that was all you needed to know; let the question pass into *argumentum ad populum*, and it will take care of itself.

In the author's experience, when the topic of home-built firearms was part of professional training, the presentation focused mainly on clandestinely modified or remade firearms, taking otherwise legal firearms and converting them to contraband items such as machine guns, short-barreled rifles, and shotguns, and the unregistered firearm suppressor. Seldom were examples cited in which persons self-made a legitimate firearm. It stands to reason that, if law-abiding, private citizens manufactured their own legal firearms, authorities would never know it existed. Authorities are tipped off and made aware as part of an investigation, meaning there is an underlying crime or at least some suspicion that there is a crime afoot.

Recall the privately made firearm movement taking shape roughly 2012–2013. During this period of time, the Bureau of Alcohol, Tobacco, Firearms and Explosives (or ATF) Firearms Technology Branch (FTB) was inundated with submitted samples accompanying requests for determinations. A letter dated December 3, 2013, sent by the ATF's FTB to the president of Tactical Innovations, Mr. Craig A. Wheatley, addresses a submitted sample of a "Ruger 10/22-type receiver." The letter affirms that the submitted sample is determined *not to* be a firearm because "the sample has not yet reached a stage in manufacture at which it would be classified as a firearm" (Griffith). Similarly, correspondence between the FTB and attorney Jason Davis on February 3, 2015, and November 2, 2015, opined to non-firearm status of three different submitted samples, a polymer AR-15 pattern receiver blank, an "AR10-type item," and a "Glock-type GC9 blank" (Curtis, 2015).

The twenty-first century is a new era with a new generation of people. This new generation is more technologically savvy and has fewer scruples when it comes to questioning the norms and traditions of the establishment and so-called conventional wisdom. The Information Age and open public accessibility to knowledge has cleared away much of the mystery, and more people have entered the conversation. As more minds began to deduce the meanings of these assemblages of words called law, they began to find activities that existing law did not address. In the classical sense of rhetoric, some would call these *loopholes* and, therefore, it is exploiting voids of gaps within the law to take advantage of it. On the other hand, some would call these non-regulated activities because the language of the law did not explicitly address them.[16] After all, there is no shortage of participants who draft the bills that could become laws. These drafters have the luxury of considerable special interest input, endless time, committees, and contemplation to ponder what activities they seek to curb or curtail, taking in the full sense of the spirit and intent of a proposed law; thus, it could be reasoned certain activities are omitted from the language law purposely, not by inadvertent oversight. This same general idea would equally apply to the promulgation of regulations which are enacted without legislative processes but none the less carry the force of law.

Long before Kevin de Leon's infamous quote in 2014 and before the term ghost guns and Cody Wilson, there was the homemade firearm. Interested parties discerned within the language of the 1968 Gun Control Act what was *not* a firearm receiver based on the language used to define a receiver. Therefore, if an object did not meet the legal definition or any definition ensconced in the promulgated regulation, it was not a receiver and, therefore, not regulated. If an object was not a firearms receiver, but was, say, a receiver blank, incomplete receiver, workpiece, or some other such term of similar meaning, it could be called something else – anything but a receiver. After all, from a practical standpoint, what would separate a piece of metal from a firearm receiver? Perhaps a few holes, some material being cut away, or other processes that transform the material into what could be defined as a *functional* or *readily restored to function* firearm receiver. This dovetails into the homemade firearm – providing the private, non-licensed individual with a non-receiver blank that is been prepared to the extent that it remains non-regulated yet simplifies the remaining work as much as possible.

Legalities and episodic impressions aside, the manufacturing of one's own firearm may also have been held in check as a matter of logistics. Until the emergence of companies offering do-it-yourself kits to simplify the build process, in order for people to manufacture their own firearms, they either had to use an existing pattern or have the ability to conceive a design then transition their ideas into a proof of concept. Once the concept and all its parts had been contemplated and proofed, the builder required access to suitable machinery and tooling to fabricate the components. This, of course, required access to raw materials from which the components were made and a good understanding of materials so that an appropriate selection would be made. If having access to tooling and materials was not enough, the builder must possess the knowledge and skill with tooling and material to actually fabricate parts. Fabricating a gun barrel, in particular, required specialized, expensive tooling and machinery to the extent that many licensed firearm manufacturers prefer to outsource barrel production to a sub-contractor rather than make their own in house. Figure 1.7 is a wartime image showing machinists fabricating barrels on lathes and is indicative of the size and scale of machinery required.

## Improvised Firearms Are Not Ghost Guns

Sometimes broadly called "zip guns," improvised firearm is a catch-all term used to describe a wide range of devices that function, even if just once, as

# A Brief History of Gun Making

**Figure 1.7** High-speed lathe operators in the plant of a large manufacturer of firearms perform precision operations on the barrels of machine guns. The plant also employs many women in turning out vital weapons for the armed forces (Image by Andreas Feininger; courtesy of Library of Congress).

a firearm, expelling a projectile under the force of an explosive. An improvised firearm can range from a crudely constructed, jury-rigged apparatus made of the most mundane, rudimentary materials using simple tools to firearms constructed of a mix of donor and homemade components, such as using a flare gun as the base from which to construct a firearm. Contextually, improvised firearms are manufactured clandestinely because of the prohibition against firearm possession or ownership. In certain extreme instances, a firearm could be improvised out of pure necessity because of the remoteness of location, poverty, or other mitigating factors that restrict routine, lawful access to commercial firearms. To facilitate the secretive nature of the improvised firearm, the most basic methods and innocuous, common materials and items are used in the construction, such as metal pipe for the receiver and barrel. The frame/receiver could be fashioned from tubing or formed using whatever metal was available to smelt – sourced from pots and pans, automotive parts, or other sources of scrap metal – that could result in a bizarre, perhaps unsafe alloy. Zip guns were seen fabricated in high school or trade school metal shops where metals could be worked and fashioned into parts. Clandestine firearm manufacturing has evolved into a fine art in many parts of the world and has been subject to several texts and documentaries.

Much of this manufacturing occurs using only the most basic hand tools and relies on the skill of the builder. The whole firearm is made of parts forged, formed, shaped, and hand assembled. Trimming and adjustment are often done with a file. Another approach is to use parts salvaged from unserviceable firearms to make a new firearm from whatever is available. Improvised firearms are a topic all unto themselves and subject to several other publications that delve deeply into the topic.

In contrast, ghost guns are not improvised firearms. The ghost gun starts with a receiver formed from an incomplete blank or one made from scratch. A ghost gun follows the patterning of an existing firearm either wholly or as inspired derivative of the existing design. Improvised firearms may rely on certain professionally made gun parts. However, ghost guns will be fully assembled into a functional firearm from the privately made receiver combined with parts made by a professional manufacturer, but this is not 100% true as lower cost, readily accessible additive manufacturing and small scale CNC machines can produce such parts.

## The Role of Technology in the Ghost Gun Debate

The effect of the internet on modern society is immeasurable. Nearly every aspect of modern life has been transformed in some way by the ever-increasing presence, accessibility, and migration of daily activities online. The internet transcends physical distance, time zones, and even language. People use the internet each and every day for education, shopping, productivity, and entertainment. The original intent of the internet's open architecture was deliberate, and its aim to be a means of sharing information in any format – text, voice, video, or imagery – quickly and seamlessly is at the very core of its purpose. If anything, what can be said about the internet is that it has democratized information, and it will remain as such as long as big tech companies and governments do not curb the free flow of all information.[17] Anyone connected to the internet potentially has access to unlimited amounts of information, of varying degrees of credibility, on demand and through devices that are more portable than ever. There is content hidden behind paywalls; however, if one knows where to look, credible, vetted information is free for the taking. Education integrates technology into learning from an early age, and people are more comfortable and fluent with technology and how to interface with it more quickly. Not only can information be shared more quickly and with greater accessibility, but also information can be instantly updated. Information, both objective and editorial, about the self-manufacture of firearms is readily accessible in not only the written word but also through audio and video demonstrations and "how-tos" as well, which were

# A Brief History of Gun Making

not possible through printed matter. Aside from access, likely the most significant concern with online content is knowing how credible it is. Anyone can publish plans online purported to create and safe and functional firearm, but a builder becomes beholden to the skills of the designer, which is often why self-made firearms follow existing patterns. Such plans are often accompanied by videos demonstrating the safety of life expectancy of the manufactured firearm.

In terms of commerce, the internet has enabled customers and vendors to more easily connect and has caused shifts in traditional supply chains. Buyers seeking to purchase regulated or non-regulated firearm components have options and are no longer limited to what local outlets may have on hand. Anything and everything can be searched, ordered, shipped, and delivered with a few clicks. Prior to the internet, there were print periodicals, books, catalogs, flyers, and other mailers that gave customers direct access to firearm vendors and their goods; however, the internet has streamlined the process considerably. Another obstacle that has been removed is supplier or manufacturer exclusivity in which, while not legally required, company practices restricted direct-to-consumer sales and pricing. If a business declines to participate in the marketplace, other companies step in to absorb the demand. In addition to mail-order catalogs and periodicals, there were publishers who specialized in content often characterized as "underground" or "counterculture" and which delved into various arts and crafts, including bombmaking, booby traps, creating new identities, escape and evasion, post-apocalyptic scenario survival, constructing improvised firearms and homemade suppressors, converting firearms to into machine guns, and so on. Perhaps one of the most famous of these was the *Anarchist's Cookbook*. The title was originally published in 1971, but it was not the only book of its type. There were literally dozens of similar books published. Books written about firearms made it very clear how to construct an expedient, or *improvised* firearm (zip guns) using basic, non-strategic materials and common household tools. Other titles showed, step by step, how to take an ordinary semi-automatic firearm and convert it into one capable of fully automatic fire. These titles were always disclaimed to have been made for informational and reference purposes only, and the reader should follow all applicable laws. A nice side effect of this printed matter is the invaluable insight it gave to firearm examiners into proposed methods for creating or altering firearms.

It is realistic to say that there is content on the internet that some find objectionable; however, in a free society, one must concede that, in order to have free speech, one must accept expressions that they may not necessarily agree with, and one's own version of protected speech cannot supersede the conflicting point of view. Conversely, simply because there is freedom of speech and expression in a free society, this in no way guarantees an audience or acceptance of what one has to say. In the case of firearm centric content, many companies and individuals have been "de-platformed" by providers who object to the subject matter. This is a debate which falls outside the scope of this text.

Technology that begat open access and democratized information has undoubtably enabled home firearm building – ready access to tools, materials, and material support and guidance. When specific resources are readily accessible through the internet, questions about the balance of free speech and safety and security concerns have arisen. To this point, the author queried "how to construct improvised explosive devices" (IEDs) through a certain widely used search engine, which returned some 11,300,000 results in less than a second. Obviously, it is impractical to look at each individual search result; however, a random selection of returns was viewed, which revealed detailed information on the precursor materials of explosive compounds and the artform of constructing such a device. The search query "how to build a gun" returned 772,000,000 returns. Some are billed as editorial and others instructional. The extent of credibility or viability of these offerings was not explored but were comprised of a blend of news reports, blogs, legal opinions, political rhetoric, and all forms of tutorials. Mind you, these were all open-source, publicly viewable materials.

The distribution of firearm designs and plans is not something that is a byproduct of the internet or a unique conception of the principles of Defense Distributed or similar parties. One merely needs to consult the U.S. Patent Office to acquire detailed plans to construct firearms and firearm centric components and accessories. For the purposes of this text, the author considers U.S. Patent #8,156,677 B2. The patent was granted on April 17, 2012, to Gaston Glock. The patent reveals detailed drawings showing the parts and inner workings of the invention, which, in this case, is a handgun. It is entirely possible that such a device could be reverse-engineered solely from diagrams. In the past, all kinds of manufactured items have been reverse-engineered from exemplars ranging from firearms to aircraft, which were deconstructed and copied, sometimes without the benefit of acknowledgment of credit or payment of royalty.

The author offers as another example in U.S. Patent 6,575,074: the Omega Firearms Suppressor. Once again, the patent, an open-source document of a protected intellectual property, details the inner workings and design of a firearm suppressor, colloquially known as a *silencer*. Should a person be so inclined, and in full violation of the patent protection, one could surreptitiously reverse-engineer the suppressor design and fabricate one clandestinely. It stands to reason, however, that if a person is willing to clandestinely construct such a device, he or she has no compunction about violating law or intellectual property rights. Even if the builder did not directly copy the depicted device, the construction and design could be used as inspiration to concoct a similar device.

It seems possible that the privately made gun movement was propelled from relative obscurity into literal headline news in 2013 when Defense Distributed published online open-source files containing plans and designs for making a functional firearm using a 3D printer. Within days, the U.S. Department of State ordered Defense Distributed to remove these plans under the pretense of a possible violation of the International Traffic in Arms Regulations (ITAR)[18]. This action may have been largely symbolic, as it is likely the files had already "gone viral" and almost certainly continued being hosted and redistributed by countless third parties through the internet and the dark web; therefore any possible hope held onto by the people behind the State Department action of stopping the redistribution of these plans is a longshot at best. While the argument was made on the basis of the ITAR violation, the action still affected interested parties within the United States because the matter involved posting and sharing the data across the internet. According to an article published online by ScienceNews, "The Liberator made a splash in 2013 when Defense Distributed, a 3-D printing and firearms company, released blueprints for the gun, the first made entirely with printable parts except for a metal nail used as the firing pin. Within a couple of days of its release, the blueprint was downloaded about 100,000 times" (Wilke, 2019). It is common knowledge that, once information is released onto the internet, it is nearly impossible to completely scrub its existence, even if there is a deliberate effort to manipulate search engine results using algorithms to suppress certain returns, hosts are shut down, or if content happens to disappear from the site. If anyone has already captured the content, it becomes a game of cat and mouse in which content is removed from one host to merely appear on another. Dark web content, by its very nature, adds a dimension of difficulty to remove.

## The Do-It-Yourself Culture

One of the prevailing cultural trends of the new millennia is the do-it-yourself (DIY) attitude – a sense of independence and individualism coupled to self-reliance. DIY was once limited to home improvement and, in fact, was facilitated largely by a series of retailers who bridged the consumer to the professional product and tools enabling the average person to fix their own toilet or install their own tile. In parallel, private gun making, like home improvement or home beer brewing, has been enabled and facilitated by the rise of companies who bridge the gap between material suppliers to the end user, coupled to the guidance to give the private party every possible chance for a successful outcome.

Firearms are durable goods. In an era of disposable, throwaway items and planned obsolescence, guns are an antithesis of these models. A firearm, properly maintained, even with normal use, can be expected to last many years. Consider the expected life expectancy of a modern major appliance and contrast that to a firearm that could become a multi-generational heirloom. The author owns firearms that are more than 100 years old. Modern consumer items, from smart phones to stoves, have realistic, expected lifespans for which it is either not economically feasible to repair or parts are no longer available, and the consumer prefers something new with all the latest and greatest features. In the case of privately made firearms, it is entirely possible the finished product is a durable good which has a theoretically indefinite lifespan. However, consider the possibility a frame or receiver is made with materials which are not durable beyond a certain calculated lifespan. In such a scenario, it may be more cost effective to simply throw away the privately made receivers when they break. A receiver made privately on a 3D printer or desktop CNC machine may cost just a few dollars to produce, so it is obviously very cost effective to simply make another receiver if one breaks.

Empirically speaking, it stands to reason that there are many factors that fuel the DIY culture. Consider the terms, "craft," "curated," "bespoke," or "small batch." These and other similar terms and phrases are almost trite from their use in advertising to describe everything and anything; hamburgers, alcoholic beverages, furniture collections, ice cream. These terms evoke a sense of individuality and create the illusion of a microcosm – attention to the smallest details and careful, deliberate selections – of anything but mass production and large corporate one size fits all products. There has always been a distinction made between the tailored suit versus one taken off the rack, but current market trends seem to insist on a tailored product with an off-the-rack price. Home gun making may be viewed as an extension of this attitude. Building one's own firearm allows for individuality and for the opportunity to put a unique artistic flare on the project. Those who fabricate their own firearms control the tolerances and quality control. They determine the finish and bring together select parts that are *curated* if you will. It could be undertaken for reasons as simple as the satisfaction of completing the project and pride of showing off the work of one's own hands. Some people simply like the challenge of undertaking new and unusual tasks. Others might be concerned about privacy and, therefore, may opt to self-manufacture their own firearm. Still others would say that they are simply exercising a right, and no further explanation or justification is necessary. Self-manufacturing does serve a legitimate educational purpose.

Gunsmithing is an accepted and even essential occupation, and fabricating a firearm gives the apprenticing smith study materials from which to learn the profession.

Artform and self-expression cannot be discounted as a core motive for self-making a firearm. Along the lines of the spirit of individuality and creativity, people may be dissatisfied with what the industry offers or may look at a complete, commercially off-the-shelf firearm as not entirely what they want. In this case, it makes sense to acquire the components to build the firearm to meet the vision of the builder and not pay for parts that are not wanted and will be replaced anyway. It is entirely possible to produce a firearm at a cost that matches or maybe even lower than a manufacturer's suggested retail price. The undertone here follows the aforementioned spirit of self-expression, individuality, and creativity, and going homemade allows builders to select and install their own parts suited to their own tastes. More than one manufacturer has gotten their start when individuals created their own firearms with their own artistic flair only to discover that they had a viable enterprise, as their product caught people's eye and a demand was created. The growth in licensed manufacturers is discussed later in this text.

On the other hand, the cost-conscious motivation may suggest flawed logic. Unless an individual intends to produce numerous firearms, it makes little financial sense to manufacture one's own firearm compared to purchasing the same type at a retail gun seller. The initial cost of even basic tooling alone can exceed the cost of a new commercially made firearm. One must still procure the materials and supplies. As more units are produced, of course, the cost of tooling and machinery is broken down over the course of the production run. In the Greenberg (2015) article cited earlier in this chapter, the costs of the three different manufacturing approaches were broken down: $1,334 using a drill press, $3,604 using a 3D printer, and $2,272 using the Ghost Gunner 3 machine. The cost of firearms fluctuates over time with various market forces, like any commodity; therefore, any figures offered are merely snapshots encapsulated at the moment. Regardless, even the cost of the Ghost Gunner 3 machine would purchase multiple firearms. The costs of 3D printers has declined considerably even since this article was written.

## The "Prepper" Movement

The "prepper" movement is one whose central theme is focused on readiness. Subscribers seek to prepare, hence "prep" themselves for theorized, anticipated forthcoming natural or manmade cataclysms. Stereotypically, the underlying concept behind prepping involves learning and honing primitive and practical skills; accumulating essentials – foodstuffs, medical supplies, and acquiring firearms and ammunition. Preppers have been characterized as a modern movement, but this is not at all accurate. Recall the months leading up to the cultish scare of Y2K and how many people responded to the "what-if" but seemingly inevitable uncertainty of a possible worldwide catastrophe when, at the stroke of midnight, the world's computers internal calendar would roll back to 1900. Before Y2K and the modern prepper movement, there were so-called "survivalists." The survivalist concept in the United States dates back at least as far as the early 1950's when civil defense authorities encouraged citizens to self-prepare under the ominous threat of a nuclear third world war. Citizens were instructed in the installation of bomb shelters in their yards, first aid, and accumulating a supply of basic essentials to form the basis of survival, food, water, medicine. From there, the survivalist idea grew and expanded to include invasion by foreign powers, suspicions of government conspiracies affecting sovereignty, false flag operations, and economic or social collapse; to name a few. Prepping is the same idea just under a different name. Call it what you will, those who subscribe to prepper ideals may gravitate to self-made firearms because of the self-reliance aspect and anonymity of possessing an officially non-existent firearm, not to mention the ability to self-make a firearm as a desirable primitive craft.

## Political Motivations

This book's introduction presented the reader with an objective political reality – the American political landscape has not as been crystal clear as political rhetoric and media talking points would have you believe, and the policy pursuits of either party do not necessarily correspond with a candidate's promises or dogmatic establishment planks on the party platform. Those of the libertarian persuasion, for example, have long advocated for deregulating firearms. Even in a broader scope outside of a firearm-specific conversation, there are people of all political persuasions who simply prefer to sidestep the establishment and avoid government interaction whenever possible. In looking at editorial remarks made by persons or "working groups" who produce plans for craft made firearms, many of them echo the same sentiments, rallying against gun control measures and asserting personal liberties. Many see the privately owned firearms as symbolic of political free speech and less as a simple pro-gun rights statement. Consider the current trends flaunted by certain venues of decriminalizing recreational narcotics or dispensing with police services running concurrently with firearms facing increasing regulations.

## The Privately Made Firearm and the Criminal Enterprise

There is ample evidence showing firearms are made privately with the intent to circumvent laws intended to prevent prohibited persons[19] from obtaining firearms. Because criminals are generally prohibited from legally obtaining or possessing firearms or ammunition, lost and stolen firearms find eager buyers on the street. According to the ATF, in 2019, there were 12,815 firearms of all types reported stolen or lost just from federal firearm licensees. Almost half the aggregate total, 6,262, were pistols (ATF, 2019).

According to a May 2019 article posted by *The Trace*, "law enforcement agencies across California are recovering record numbers of ghost guns. According to the ATF, 30 percent of all guns now recovered by agents in the state are unserialized" (Stephens, 2019). The article cites several examples of unserialized firearms being used in high-profile shooting incidents in California and indicates that the number of unserialized firearm seizures is increasing. In at least two of the cases cited, the shooter was either denied a retail firearm purchase or would have been denied the sale because of criminal history or other prohibitors *under existing laws*. It stands to reason that, if an individual is already prohibited from possessing a firearm, his or her focus will be on acquiring replacement firearms from any source that presents itself. It is also worth considering that criminals themselves are interested in avoiding attention and controlling the risk of exposure. It could then be reasoned that a prohibited person may attempt to produce his or her own firearm clandestinely instead of attempting to obtain a firearm on the street. However, because many may lack the ability or mere motivation to assemble their own firearms, they may turn to outside builders who could act as a conduit to supply firearms for such parties.[20] Either way, the firearm is simply a means to justify an end, regardless of its sourcing and without considering the law. As long as criminals are willing to gamble on the chance that they are not going to get caught or, if apprehended, will beat the charges, laws are transparent to the violator.

An article posted on *The Daily Beast* on January 2, 2020, titled, "Couple Gets Engaged, Uses 3D Gun to Murder Ex's Mom: Cops" claimed that a 3D-printed firearm was used to commit a homicide in Rhode Island. "Detective Sgt. Christopher LeFort of the Pawtucket Major Crimes Square said investigators are still examining the murder weapon, 'but it does appear to be 3D-printed'" (Connor, 2020). A subsequent story published by *Patch* further described the gun, short of declaring it a 3D-printed firearm,

> According to police, the gun has a polymer frame and no serial numbers on the frame, slide or barrel. The slide was made by Rock Island Armory. The gun is fully functional, police said, and fired without incident at the lab.

**(Nunes, 2020)**[21]

A July 15, 2020, press release issued by the U.S. Attorney's Office Eastern District of Virginia announced the arraignment of 20-year-old Davud Sungur. Sungur is accused of selling, among other items, "ghost guns" and, "Sungur allegedly also sold detectives devices he claimed to have made using a 3D printer that, after installation, would enable semi-automatic firearms to fire fully automatically".[22] The press release reports a 3D printer was seized along with other evidence during the execution of a search warrant on the defendant's residence (U.S. Attorney's Office, 2020). In addition to the evidence accumulated during the controlled buy, the 3D printer, the files onboard the printer or peripheral devices, and any communications to set up the deals are all going to be compelling evidence in this matter.

## Brain Trust: Potential Benefits of Self-Manufactured Firearms

A significant point that has been overlooked in the debate over self-made firearms is the potential contribution a person could make to the national defense. Consider the unnamed, unknown person – a thinker/tinkerer who develops an idea or improves upon an existing idea – whose principal beneficiary could be the armed forces. There is a long and storied tradition of inventors and thinkers pioneering a novel concept completely on their own that had great strategic value. It is perhaps within this spirit that U.S. law never addressed self-made, non-regulated firearms, leaving leeway for one of the most endearing aspects of the American experience – innovation. Some may argue that this was an oversight or a "loophole" in the law; however, it seems hard to believe all those legislative committees and congressional aides and staffers, assisted by endless consultants, advisors, and lobbyists who regulate for a living, would write volumes of law and regulation but somehow overlook the homemade firearm while regulating every other firearm. There is a lot to be said for independent thinkers outside of the establishment who come into a problem offering a different perspective. Simply stated, there is more potential for development simply because more persons are involved, not just those employed by governments or by arms makers themselves. In 1986 manufacturing machine guns for private sale was legally prohibited; and this had the net effect of a real "brain drain" on the small arms industry. Because private persons, and any entity not licensed to engage in manufacturing of automatic firearms are prohibited from creating a physical proof of concept (which could be construed as manufacturing a machine gun), this has prevented anyone from doing anything other than imagining a new firearm system.[23] The author offers the arguement that the development of a new generation of small arms has been stymied by the lack of broader, democratic participation. We can only theorize how national defense could have benefited from an individual who could have devised the next evolution in military small arms, had they not been prohibited by laws from doing so. This line of thinking has been fully proven by the advancements in just the last twenty years in firearm suppressor technology. While suppressors are regulated, a non-licensed person can still make one insomuch as the application is filed, approved, and the payment of tax is made. Laws have consequences which are not limited to punishing the offender or impeding free actions by free peoples.

## Notes

1. For comparison, NORINCO, North China Industries, is owned by the Chinese government. Austrian company GLOCK Ges.m.b.H. is privately held. The U.S. government operated a series of arsenals until finally closing the last one, the Springfield Arsenal, in 1968.
2. A carbine is a shortened version of a full-length rifle. The functional characteristics remains the same, but the overall length, barrel length, and mass are reduced to create a lighter, handier firearm.
3. During the Second World War, the U.S. Army Ordnance Corps issued contracts to manufacture M-1 carbines to ten primary companies, nine of which were not arms manufacturers and had no background in arms making. Winchester Repeating Arms was the only exception. The wartime production spanned approximately 38 months, and some 6,221,220 carbines were manufactured. This averages out to almost four guns per minute, 24 hours a day, for the duration of the production run.
4. Armalite was formed with the intention of acting as a think tank with a focus on creating state-of-the-art small arms. The company did not have any intention of actually manufacturing firearms but, instead, selling licenses for its designs to established manufacturers.
5. The AR-15 was the predecessor to the M16, the U.S. Army designation for the firearm when it was accepted into military service. The design. by then. had passed from Armalite to Colt. Much later, the AR-10 would be accepted into U.S. military service as a sniper rifle.
6. The author uses this year because it coincides with the sunset of the Public Safety and Recreational Firearms Use Protection Act. This act was part of Public Law 103-322, the Violent Crime Control and Law Enforcement Act of 1994.
7. On December 18, 2020, the ATF announced intentions to proceed with Objective Factors for Classifying Weapons With "Stabilizing Braces" (85 FR 82516) as a "final guidance document." As required, the proposal was published in the Federal Register and was opened to public comment. Subsequently, on December 31, 2020, this proposal was withdrawn by the ATF, citing "further review from the Justice Department" as a rationale. According to the posting on the Federal Register, as of January 24, 2021, there

had been 393,068 page views and 73,536 comments made. A brief review of random postings, which are public, the author did not find one comment supporting this proposal. In June 2021 ATF published proposal ATF 2021R-08 to address braced equipped handguns once again. As proposed, the government would use a worksheet (ATF 4999) with point scoring system to determine if a brace equipped firearm is a rifle or "braced handgun". Public comment period for this proposal closed on September 8, 2021. According to the *Regulations.gov* page statistics 209,044 comments were recorded in response to the rulemaking change.

8. Firearm types are defined in Chapter 4.
9. See classification letter to Mossberg dated March 2, 2017 from the ATF Firearms Technology Industry Services Branch concerning the Mossberg Shockwave classification as a firearm under the Gun Control Act but not under the National Firearms Act. The letter makes reference to similarly configured firearms that had also been reviewed.
10. See letter dated December 14, 2018, between Dan O'Kelly (International Firearm Specialist Academy) and Franklin Armory published on the Franklin Armory website concerning ATF Firearms Technology Industry Services Branch determinations made on submitted exemplar firearms for classification.
11. Caliber is the size of ammunition cartridge expressed as a decimal, and customarily accompanied by an identifier, i.e. .45 ACP of .45 Auto.
12. A *clip* is a firearm ammunition storage device but is often confused with a magazine, which is a different article altogether. A *clip* is used to load a *magazine*.
13. For comparison, the M134, a 7.52×51mm six-barreled gatling gun, has an adjustable rate of fire up to about 6,000 rounds per minute, some 100 rounds per second.
14. A logical fallacy, as correlation does not imply causation.
15. Both types of firearms are regulated under the National Firearms Act. This topic is explored in greater detail later in this text.
16. These may be viewed, depending on one's point of view, as positive or negative rights.
17. In light of recent revelations there has been more attention to how internet search results are manipulated through algorithms, which affects how readily, if at all, certain content is revealed. De-platforming eliminates content altogether, and throttling inhibits accessibility to content.
18. International Arms Trafficking Regulations. The U.S. State Department's Directorate of Defense Trade Controls oversees the administration of the body of regulations and must approve the exportation of certain military articles and technology. ITAR is interpreted broadly and can include seemingly benign articles such as optical scopes. Alleged ITAR violations have even included radios and radio technical data (U.S. Department of State Concludes $13 Million Settlement of Alleged Export Violations by L3Harris Technologies, Inc., September 23, 2019) (U.S. Department of State, n.d.)
19. A prohibited person is generally defined as persons who are convicted felons whose rights have not been restored, adjudicated mentally incompetent, and subject to certain court orders or other conditions and situations that would prevent a person from lawfully obtaining a firearm.

20. Such activities would be unlawful. Manufacturing firearms for sale is strictly limited to licensed manufacturers. Such illicit sales could include any kind of firearm, regardless of origin.
21. The State of Rhode Island criminalized ghost guns, such as 3D-printed firearms, in June 2020. In the quote from the story, police describe a slide marked "Rock Island Armory." This suggests the device was an automatic pistol and likely a 1911 pattern. Rock Island Armory is a recognized brand made for Armscor and manufactures 1911 style pistols. The frame of the exhibit firearm could be homemade and coupled to commercially made parts.
22. The author believes the device described here is a drop-in auto sear, which serves the functional purpose of converting a semi-automatic firearm into one capable of operating as a fully automatic firearm. A drop-in auto sear is depicted in this text, Figure 3.4.
23. John Garand, creator of the M1 Garand, was not a government employee when he devised the gun that bears his name. Only later was he given a government job to justify his continued work on refining the design. John Browning was not employed by the government either, yet the U.S. government was an eager customer for his independently created designs. Under current gun laws, it is likely at least some of Browning's designs would have never seen fruition. In the current conversation, both men would have been making ghost guns.

## References

ATF. (2019). *Federal Firearms Licensee (FFL) Theft/Loss Report*. U.S. Department of Justice.

Connor, T. (2020, January 2). Couple Gets Engaged, Uses 3D Gun to Murder Ex's Mom: Cops. Retrieved July 18, 2020, from *The Daily Beast*: https://www.thedailybeast.com/police-charge-jack-doherty-and-shaylyn-moran-with-murdering-woman-with-3d-printed-gun?ref=scroll

Curtis, M. R. (2015, November 2). Product Determination Letters. Retrieved July 26, 2020, from *Polymer 80.com Media*: https://www.polymer80.com/media/wysiwyg/porto/LegalDocs/P80_Product_Determination_Letters.pdf

Defense Distributed. (n.d.). About. Retrieved July 5, 2020, from *Defense Distributed*: https://defdist.org

Greenberg, A. (2015, June 3). I Made an Untraceable AR-15 "Ghost Gun" in My Office—and It Was Easy. *Wired*. Retrieved from https://www.wired.com/2015/06/i-made-an-untraceable-ar-15-ghost-gun/

Griffith, E. (n.d.). Pike Arms® ELITE22™ "80 Percent" Receiver Blank ATF Approved – No FFL Required. Retrieved July 25, 2020, from *Tactical Innovations*: https://www.tacticalinc.com/catalog/product/id-3899

Nunes, R. (2020, January 13). Pawtucket Shooting Mystery: Was Gun 3D-Printed? Retrieved July 18, 2020, from *Patch.com*: https://patch.com/rhode-island/cranston/pawtucket-shooting-mystery-was-gun-3d-printed

Stealth Arms. (n.d.). About. Retrieved July 13, 2020, from *Stealtharms*: https://www.stealtharms.net/about-stealth-arms

Stephens, A. (2019, May 17). Ghost Guns Are Everywhere in California. Retrieved July 13, 2020, from *The Trace*: https://www.thetrace.org/2019/05/ghost-gun-california-crime/

U.S. Attorney's Office. (2020, July 15). Alleged Dealer of Ghost Guns and Machinegun Conversion Devices Arraigned. Retrieved July 25, 2020, from *Justice.gov*: https://www.justice.gov/usao-edva/pr/alleged-dealer-ghost-guns-and-machinegun-conversion-devices-arraigned

Wilke, C. (2019, September 24). 3-D Printed "Ghost Guns" Pose New Challenges for Crime-Scene Investigators. Retrieved July 18, 2020, from *ScienceNews*: https://www.sciencenews.org/article/3d-printed-guns-plastic-ballistics-crime

# Regulated and Non-Regulated Manufacturing

## 2

### DOES AN INDIVIDUAL NEED A LICENSE TO MAKE A FIREARM FOR PERSONAL USE?

No, a license is not required to make a firearm solely for personal use. However, a license is required to manufacture firearms for sale or distribution. The law prohibits a person from assembling a non-sporting semiautomatic rifle or shotgun from 10 or more imported parts, as well as firearms that cannot be detected by metal detectors or x-ray machines. In addition, the making of an NFA firearm requires a tax payment and advance approval by ATF.

[18 U.S.C. 922(o), (p) and (r); 26 U.S.C. 5822; 27 CFR 478.39, 479.62 and 479.105]

(ATF, 2017)

## Regulated and Non-Regulated Firearm Manufacturing Activity

Under current federal law, and as published by the Bureau of Alcohol, Tobacco and Explosives (ATF), the private individual is not required to acquire nor maintain a firearms manufacturer's license to *self-manufacture* a firearm solely for personal use as long as certain conditions met. The ultimate legality of self-manufacturing and its final products is subject to conditions, including the type of firearm constructed, the materials[1] used in the construction, the limited use of imported parts (not accessories) to construct such a firearm, and that the individual is not prohibited from possessing a firearm. The private individual who manufactures a firearm for **personal use** is deemed *non-regulated activity*. Because it is non-regulated activity, there cannot be any enforceable, federally mandated[2] requirements to mark or engrave the receiver with identifying information or report its existence to any third party. This is also true for ammunition manufactured by a private individual

DOI: 10.4324/9781003044499-2

for personal consumption; under current federal law, such activities are not regulated, nor is manufacturer licensing required.[3] Within the language of ATF 2021R-05, a series of proposed rules would redefine a firearm frame or receiver, it is articulated, "nothing in this rule would restrict persons not otherwise prohibited from possessing firearms making their own firearms at home without markings solely for personal use" (ATF, 2021).

With the growth of interest in privately made arms, it is almost inevitable that situations arise in which there are ambiguities or a lack of definitive guidance. Concerned parties, who are interested in following the law, go to the regulators; who may address the question through regulatory interpretation. If this is an imperfect solution, or the interpretation could be argued as being inconsistent with existing laws from which regulation is derived, the matter is then litigated thru the court. For example, ATF Ruling 2015-1 (published January 2, 2015) sought to clarify participation in the activity of "manufacturing a firearm frame or receiver" and itself was a revision of a prior ruling, ATF 2010-10. In part, 2010-10 addressed the scope and practice of the licensed gunsmith/retail firearms dealer. It has long been the customary role of the gunsmith to repair, maintain, adorn, and modify *existing* firearms. All of which were consistent with an understanding that the work being performed was on behalf of a customer. However, the language of 2015-1, someone felt it important it be clarified the gunsmith performed work on *existing* firearms – the gunsmith does not own the firearm, is not making a new firearm, and is not selling or distributing the firearm for profit or gain in their business practice; in other words essentially engaging in manufacture rather then work on an existing firearm. To this point, review Figure 2.1, which depicts a functional Kimber 8400 Magnum receiver. The builder would attach a suitable barrel and bed the action into a stock at the

**Figure 2.1** A fully functional Kimber Model 8400 Magnum receiver. Because this receiver is functional in its present state, the sale is regulated as a firearm even though it lacks a stock and barrel (Image courtesy of Kimber America).

**Figure 2.2** A fully assembled rifle using a Kimber Model 8400 Magnum receiver, as seen in Figure 2.1. The receiver has been barreled and set into a stock. The rifle is now fully assembled and ready to use (Image courtesy of Kimber America).

customer's request. Figure 2.2 depicts a similar barreled action that has been set and bedded into a stock to form the completed build. Customizing, tuning, or completing such builds for customers is a common practice for gunsmiths. The gunsmith did not create the receiver; a licensed manufacturer did, so the gunsmith only needed to make improvements to it.

Ruling 2015-1 also clarified another point: home builders need their own tools to fabricate their own frames/receivers and cannot rely on or utilize the resources under the control of an outside entity to create their frames/receivers. Thus, renting machinery, attending so-called "build parties," or belonging to "gun clubs," which give individuals access to other's machinery and tooling, is a prohibited practice. Anything that builders use, they themselves must possess or have articulable dominion over. An unfortunate consequence of cracking down on build parties or gun clubs is the rise of inherently dangerous homemade firearms; absent oversight, guidance, and materials offered in such environments, many would-be home builders have concocted dangerous articles because of lack of skill, improper tools, poor material selection, and overall build quality.

It might be a coincidence that, on October 2, 2014, some two months prior to ATF Ruling 2015-1, the United States Attorney's Office for the Central District of California announced the indictment of Joseph Roh "on a federal charge related to the illegal manufacture and sale of lower receivers for AR-15-type rifles, as well as completed firearms" (Department of Justice, 2014).[4] According to the information contained in the U.S. Department of Justice's (DOJ) press release, Roh operated an Orange County, California, machine shop,

> Roh attempted to avoid the licensing requirement by requiring that each customer play a token role in the manufacturing process, which often meant merely pushing a button on a CNC machine, while company employees did the vast majority of the work. While the sale of unfinished lower receivers is not regulated, the manufacture and sale of completed lower receivers – which are considered firearms under federal law – requires a proper license.

Essentially, Roh was accused of acting as a manufacturer because he allowed persons into his machine shop where they would fabricate a receiver using

Roh's machinery. ATF did not deem the pressing of a button to initiate the CNC machine to undertake the process of transforming a blank into a receiver to be within the law concerning a non-licensed entity manufacturing their own firearm for personal use.

At face value, the case would appear to be fairly straightforward with an easily proven allegation, inasmuch as a jury would be persuaded by the government's argument[5] – Roh was not a licensed manufacturer but was alleged to be engaging in the manufacturing and distributing of firearms.

> A business (including an association or society) may not avoid the manufacturing license, marking, and recordkeeping requirements of the GCA by allowing persons to perform manufacturing processes on firearms (including frames or receivers) using machinery or equipment under its dominion and control where that business controls access to, and use of, such machinery or equipment.
>
> (ATF, 2015)

However, the case took a rather unusual turn which had broader implications. The defense challenged the government's case on the basis that the AR-15 lower receiver, the type of firearm Roh was accused of manufacturing, was not definable as a firearm receiver because it lacked certain characteristics used to define a receiver[6]: "That part of a firearm which provides housing for the hammer, bolt or breechblock, and firing mechanism, and which is usually threaded at its forward portion to receive the barrel" (ATF, 2019).[7] In the case of the AR-15-style lower receiver, there is no accommodation to attach or contain the bolt or breechblock, nor is it threaded at its forward portion to receive the barrel. The case was resolved by a brokered plea arrangement between prosecutors and Roh. A video on YouTube and broadcast on May 16, 2016, by KPIX, a San Francisco-area CBS affiliate, shows some of the footage captured by undercover agents inside Roh's operation.[8] One of the changes in verbiage within the ATF 2021R-05 proposal to is redefine frames and receivers. The document cites the Roh case specifically, almost with a tone of lamentation, going so far as to suggest,"(T)hese courts' interpretation of ATF regulations, if broadly followed, could mean as many as 90 percent of all firearms now in the United States would not have any frame or receiver subject to regulation" (ATF, 2021). The author finds this assertion hyperbolic, if not absurdly ridicoulous. Such a claim is not realistic given extensive, existing case law; let alone generally accepted practice within the industry. The government argument pretends the same types of receivers it claims may not fit existing regulatory language did not exist at the time the Gun Control Act was enacted (1968). On page five of the document there are several examples of firearms cited – the AR-15–style rifle, Glock- and SIG-type semi automatic pistols, and especially with respect to the Glock design as a strike fired pistol

# Regulated and Non-Regulated Manufacturing

thus having no hammer. It is as if the semi automatic pistol with a separate slide and frame did not exist at the time the original law was written, when in fact such automatic pistols had been in existance for some 70 years. Striker-fired, hammerless pistols had existed for some 60 years. The AR-type bifurcated receiver had been in existance since the mid 1950s, and was the standard U.S. military rifle when the Gun Control Act was written, notwithstanding other bifurcated receiver designs also in existance, so it was not a secret when the Act was contemplated. A possible argument is made for the SIG, with its lower grip module.[9] It is hard to believe these firearms could not have been considered when the Gun Control Act was written and debated. So, we are left with two possible conclusions – either the Gun Control Act is bad law because it is incomplete in scope or was incompetently written and signed into effect; or subsequent interpretations of the Gun Control Act are erroneous because such interpretations are not present within the language of the act. None the less, if such drastic changes to language are needed to address what apparently were oversights, perhaps it is best served by the legislative process of lawmaking rather than by a regulatory action.

## Regulated Firearms Manufacturing Activity in the United States

According to the ATF, in 2018, licensed firearm manufacturers in the United States produced 9,052,628 firearms. Of those, 554,237 firearms were exported. There were 4,305,851 firearms imported into the United States from sources offshore.[10] In sum, during 2018, 12,804,242 firearms remained within or entered the United States through routine commercial channels (ATF, 2020). Figure 2.3 represents the 5-year manufacturing and importation trends to

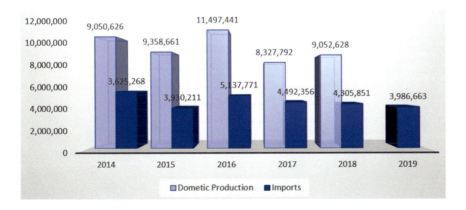

**Figure 2.3** United States firearms commerce 2013–2019.

better illustrate this data. Firearm production numbers were reported by federally licensed manufacturers, while imports and exports were handled by licensed entities engaged in those activities.

## Growth Trend in Licensed Manufacturers

According to the ATF, since 1974, the number of federally licensed firearm manufacturers has steadily increased. In 2013, there were 9,094 licensees. By 2019, the number had grown to 13,044 licensees, an increase of 3,950 licensees, some 30%. Interestingly, historical licensing data reveals that there were fewer than 1,000 licensed firearm manufacturers in the United States from 1974 to 1991.[11] There is no distinction drawn in the size or scope of licensed manufacturers, it is only to state an entity is licensed to manufacture; thus, firearms manufacturers range in size from sole proprietorships to large operations who employ hundreds of people and who are easily recognized household names. For context, in 2018, Sturm, Ruger, and Company Inc. in Newport, Hew Hampshire, reported manufacturing 447,736[12] rifles, while AK-USA Manufacturing,[13] based in Fort Myers, Florida, reported manufacturing four rifles that same year. Figure 2.4 illustrates the overall growth trend in licensed firearm manufacturers in the United States between 2013 and 2018.

When comparing manufacturing activity on the part of licensed entities to the increasing number of licensed manufacturers, it is apparent that the increasing interest in non-regulated firearm manufacturing has little, if any, effect on commerce for existing manufacturers and has not deterred interested parties from obtaining licensure and entering the industry. When the

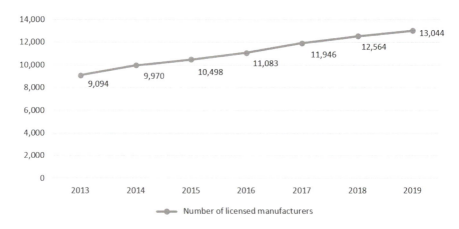

**Figure 2.4** Licensed firearm manufacturers within the United States.

number of imported firearms is contemplated, this disparity becomes even more apparent because, during any given year, imports account for roughly one-third of the firearms entering commerce in the United States. It is interesting to contemplate the number of persons who engaged in non-regulated activity and then decided to seek licensure and expand their craft into a commercial enterprise.

## 2020 into 2021 Firearm Sales Trends

Preliminary figures on the U.S. firearm sales report nearly 40 million firearms were sold in 2020. The breakdown and, therefore, the ratio of imported to domestically made firearms is not established. According to an article published by the Brookings Institute, which used data obtained from the FBI NICS[14] statistics, "Our estimates indicate that almost three million more firearms have been sold since March than would have ordinarily been sold during these months. Half of that increase occurred in June alone" and,

> On March 13, President Trump issued a proclamation declaring a national emergency concerning the COVID-19 outbreak. Over the next 12 days (including that day), firearm sales surged, jumping to over 120,000 per day, and peaking at 176,000 on March 16. Over 700,000 additional firearms were sold in March.
>
> **(Levine & McKnight, 2020)**

Mirroring this analysis from Brookings, *The Daily Caller* reported that,

> So far in 2020, three months have sported over 3 million NICS background checks, more than any previous month since the FBI began recording the statistics 22 years ago in 1998. March saw 3.7 million checks May say [sic] 3.1 million, and June 3.9 million.
>
> **(Hagstrom, 2020)**

The net result of this growth in sales has put a tremendous strain on the supply chain, which has affected not only licensed manufacturers but also the outlets that supply non-regulated builders as well. The author looked into numerous sites and discovered that many outlets were out of stock on supplies for private gun making, some with indeterminate back-order status, stemming from a combination of demand for parts outweighing supply and mandated workplace shutdowns due to the coronavirus outbreak. Many licensed retail firearm dealers sat with empty shelves awaiting orders to be fulfilled. So far as manufacturers are concerned, many added forth shifts in order to increase production and were running 24 hours per day. The lifespan of this upward trend in firearms sales remains to be seen, but according to the FBI NICS statistics the trend continued through July and August, with 3,639,224 and 3,115,063 background checks run, respectively, and a total of 25,934,334 NICS background checks run in the first 8 months of 2020, a number that has already exceeded the total figure for gun sales in 2017 (FBI, 2020). The uncertainty of the U.S. 2020 general election[15] seems to have continued to fuel the demand for firearms so, in real terms, a customer enters a retail sales establishment and faces nearly empty shelves and few choices. According to an article published online by *Forbes*, "The FBI reported that background checks for firearms purchases exceeded 4.31 million in January. That is the largest monthly tally since the FBI started keeping track in 1998, and the first time the count has topped 4 million" (Smith, 2021). If this trajectory were maintained month to month in 2021, nearly 52,000,000 firearms would be sold.[16]

## Opposition to Non-Regulated Manufacturing

On July 1, 2018, California Penal Code sections 29180–29184 went into effect. The law requires residents who self-manufacture or self-assemble a firearm to apply for a unique serial number *prior* to undertaking those steps, if the firearm was not already serialized or other identifying markings were affixed. The act also requires persons newly residing in California to do the same if they establish residency while possessing firearms that were self-manufactured or self-assembled, even though the activity occurred outside the state of California. Law cannot be contemplated in a vacuum and ignore the existence of other, possibly concurrent laws. Consider this point – whether by design or an unintended consequence, the state of California maintains a roster of handguns legal for sale, and handguns that do not appear on the roster are not approved for sale within California. Within the scope of both laws, it has been suggested the California Department of Justice would not approve any applications for a self-manufactured or self-assembled handgun and, therefore, would decline to issue a unique serial number to this homemade handgun because such a handgun would not be listed on the California sale-approved roster.[17]

On September 29, 2020, the state of California, partnering with co-plaintiffs, brought a suit[18] against the ATF and other federal entities. The suit alleges that the ATF is in error with its determination of 80% receivers as non-gun, non-regulated articles under language expressed in the 1968 *Gun Control Act*. The plaintiffs claim such an item is a firearm as defined because, in their estimation, it is a frame readily made to function. Within the language of the suit is found this remark:

> For any and all of these reasons, this Court should vacate ATF's determinations and direct ATF in the future to classify 80 percent receivers for what they are: lethal weapons subject to federal firearms statutes and regulations.

**(Complaint for Declaratory and Injunctive Relief, 2020)**

Compare this suit to California's own requirements to register a self-made firearm. One seems to contradict the other – on the one hand, they offer a path to lawfully make such a firearm, but then, on the other hand, file a lawsuit against the United States to ban the same articles, effectively negating the legal path by state registration. One cannot help but ponder whether this is tantamount to an admission of the ineffectiveness or impracticality of the law,[19] but one thing is clear: the apparent interest by the state of California to compel an agency of the U.S. government to change its policy while concurrently ignoring other existing laws of the same government.

A similar lawsuit was brought by the city of Syracuse, New York, and others[20] against the ATF, using much the same argument as the California case and even some of the same verbiage, as both cases generously sprinkle the phrase, "arbitrary and capricious" in their written argument. Court actions have brought actions against individual corporations by governments, such as the District of Columbia's suit against Polymer80.

Other state governments, including Connecticut,[21] Washington, and Rhode Island have taken similar legislative action to regulate non-licensed manufacturing or assembly of firearms. Hawaii, New York, and New Jersey have banned the practice entirely. Connecticut, like California, requires the fabricator to obtain a unique serial number from the state and engrave said number on the receiver. Unlike California, however, the Connecticut law stipulates that the identification number must be obtained subsequent to manufacture. Some state laws reach further and prohibit the sale of certain tooling and machinery that they connect to self-manufacturing firearms, even if such items may have other, non-firearm, applications.

In December 2018,[22] the Brady Campaign to Prevent Gun Violence brought suit against the U.S. Department of State over the reversal of its official stance on the question of 3D-printed firearms. As discussed in Chapter 1 of this text, in 2013, the U.S. Department of State took legal action against Defense Distributed over online publishing of plans and schematics to produce firearms using 3D printers. The State Department later ceased litigation and reached a settlement with Defense Distributed. However, this was not the end of the story, as this prompted several states and commonwealths to bring suit against Defense Distributed concerning these plans.[23] The Brady Campaign to Prevent Gun Violence makes this assertion:

> The 3D printing of firearms is a severely dangerous threat to American safety. With the blueprints of firearms available online, anyone – a terrorist or any prohibited purchaser – can obtain a fully functioning firearm without a background check though the use of 3D printer.
>
> **(Brady Campaign to Prevent Gun Violence, 2018)**

Both houses with the United States Congress, the House of Representatives and the Senate have both seen bills, which are virtually mirrors of one another, introduced to address the question of 3D printing and the sharing of data files to make printed firearms.

In May, 2021 the ATF released 2021R-05 titled *Definition of "Frame or Receiver" and Identification of Firearms* proposing new rules and amendments to existing rules. The proposal does not dispense with the practice of self-made firearms, which would be termed as "Privately Made Firearms" but does add certain caveats to the practice and expands the meaning of the term receiver, among other initiatives contained within the language; primarily among them reclassifying what were formally known as receiver blanks or 80% receivers as part of "firearm receiver kits" as receivers. There is no reason to doubt these proposals as stated will go forward and become ensconced into regulation.

## Legalities Affecting the Final Configuration of Self-Made Firearms

If an individual self-manufactures a firearm frame/receiver, there is still the question of the final configuration of the wholly assembled firearm. As discussed in this chapter, certain individual states mandate declaration and registration of homemade frames/receivers under force of law, but there is a secondary question beyond the mere making of the receiver. Outside of the actual fabrication of the frame/receiver, the builder selects what type of firearm the final iteration of the project will take on. This portion of the assembly brings with it a completely new set of rules to remain in legal compliance with federal law let alone any possible state laws. U.S. Code defines the type of firearms based upon certain present characteristics as assembled. In the past, a firearm frame or receiver was specifically formed for a certain type of firearm; however, in contemporary times, the frame/receiver could be manufactured into a plurality of different types, which gives the builder the option of different types inasmuch as they are legally compliant. California, for example, places strict stipulations on the features and characteristics that can be present on a rifle, including styles of stock, forward grips, flash suppressor, and the ability to accept a detachable magazine, among others. Pistols and shotguns also have certain caveats concerning features as well. Outside of California, such restrictions do not exist; however, the type of firearm constructed must be legally compliant with U.S. Code and the relevant regulations.

## Firearm Types and Definitions[24]

When the receiver is complete, the builder assembles the other requisite parts to this receiver, including a barrel, fire control parts, safety mechanism, grips, and so forth, to make the firearm wholly completed. Like any hobby or interest, it is possible, if not inevitable, that one will accumulate parts and spares that *could* be used to assemble a plurality of configurations and types of firearms. The home builder must be cautious with respect to how they have configured their final assembly inasmuch as it is a legal configuration. In January 1992, the U.S. Supreme Court heard arguments in the matter of *United States v. Thompson/Center Arms Company*.[25] Essentially, the government's argument was that a firearm "kit" manufactured and sold by Thompson/Center Arms Company as the Contender model provided the buyer the ready means to assemble an unregistered short-barreled rifle using the parts provided in said "kit." The classification would restrict the sale of the Contender as an NFA-regulated firearm and require payment of tax. During the government's oral arguments, the justices were quick to clarify that the pieces and parts contained within the kit could be used to assemble a firearm not subject to regulatory provisions in the NFA. It seems, therefore, without the literal verbiage, the government's argument was solely predicated on the point that a person simply could not resist the temptation to assemble an unregistered short-barreled rifle if they had the means at hand to do so, nor would they voluntarily file the necessary documents to lawfully make a short-barreled rifle if one were desired. This argument unmistakably runs contrary to a presumption of innocence, a baseline of the standards of American justice, akin to a person who buys a sports car is assumed to inevitably exceed speed limits, drive recklessly, and ultimately cause an accident, resulting in property damage, injuries, and death. None of these assumptions are in evidence. The Supreme Court ruled in favor of Thompson/Center Arms Company. Although decided on June 8, 1992, it was not until July 25, 2011, that the ATF published a ruling that cited the Thompson decision[26] concerning assemblage of parts.

Any Other Weapon: Any weapon or device capable of being concealed on the person from which a shot can be discharged through the energy of an explosive; a pistol or revolver having a barrel with a smooth bore designed or redesigned to fire a fixed shotgun shell; weapons with combination shotgun and rifle barrels of 12 inches or more that are less than 18 inches in length from which only a single discharge can be made from either barrel without manual reloading; and any such weapon that may be readily restored to fire. The term "any other weapon" shall not include a pistol or a revolver with a rifled bore or bores or weapons designed, made, or intended to be fired from the shoulder and are not capable of firing fixed ammunition. Figure 2.5 depicts a smooth-bore handgun as an example of an "any other weapon."

Destructive Device: (a) Any explosive, incendiary, or poison gas (1) bomb, (2) grenade, (3) rocket with a propellent charge of more than 4 ounces, (4) missile with an explosive or incendiary charge of more than one-quarter ounce, (5) mine, or (6) similar device; (b) any type of weapon by whatever name that will or may be readily converted to expel a projectile by the action of an explosive or other propellant, the barrel or barrels of which have a bore of more than one-half inch in diameter, except a shotgun or shotgun shell that the director finds is generally recognized as particularly suitable for sporting purposes; and (c) any combination of parts either designed or intended for use in converting any device into a destructive device as described in paragraphs (a) and (b) of this definition and from which a destructive device may be readily assembled. The term "destructive device" shall not include any device that is neither designed nor redesigned for use as a weapon; any device, although originally designed for use as a weapon, that is redesigned for use as a signaling, pyrotechnic, line throwing, safety, or similar device; surplus ordnance sold, loaned, or given by the Secretary of the Army under 10 U.S.C. 4684(2), 4685, or 4686; or any device that the director finds is not

**Figure 2.5** The Remington modular combat shotgun. This firearm is a registered on the National Firearms Act as an "any other weapon," as it meets the definition of a smooth-bored handgun (Image by Phil Puglisi; used with permission).

# Regulated and Non-Regulated Manufacturing

likely to be used as a weapon, is an antique, or is a rifle that the owner intends to use solely for sporting purposes.

Frame or Receiver: The part of a firearm that provides the housing for the hammer, bolt or breechblock, and firing mechanism and that is usually threaded at its forward portion to receive the barrel. Refer to Figure 2.1, which shows a receiver absent of a barrel and other parts as a fully assembled firearm. The meaning of the terms frame or receiver are set to be greatly expanded under ATF 2021R-05.

Machine Gun: Any weapon that shoots, is designed to shoot, or can be readily restored to shoot, automatically more than one shot, without manual reloading, by a single function of the trigger. The term "machine gun" shall also include the frame or receiver of any such weapon; any part designed and intended solely and exclusively or combination of parts designed and intended for use in converting a weapon into a machine gun; and any combination of parts from which a machine gun can be assembled if such parts are in the possession or under the control of a person. For purposes of this definition, the term "**automatically**," as it modifies "**shoots, is designed to shoot, or can be readily restored to shoot**," means functioning as the result of a self-acting or self-regulating mechanism that allows the firing of multiple rounds through a single function of the trigger; and "**single function of the trigger**" means a single pull of the trigger and analogous motions. The term "machine gun" includes a bump-stock-type device,[27] i.e., a device that allows a semi-automatic firearm to shoot more than one shot with a single pull of the trigger by harnessing the recoil energy of the semi-automatic firearm to which it is affixed so that the trigger resets and continues firing without additional physical manipulation of the trigger by the shooter. Figure 2.6 depicts a machine gun receiver (Figure 2.6).

Muffler or silencer: Any device for silencing, muffling, or diminishing the report of a portable firearm, including any combination of parts, designed or redesigned, intended for the use in assembling or fabricating a firearm silencer or firearm muffler and any part intended for use only in such assembly or fabrication. Proposed rules under ATF2021R-05 would amend this slightly by clarifying not all parts need to be marked, only the body or housing, unless the smaller parts, i.e., baffles and the like, are independent of a complete device are disposed of. See Figure 2.7 for an example of a wholly complete firearm suppressor.

Pistol: A weapon originally designed, made, and intended to fire a projectile (bullet) from one or more barrels when held in one hand that has (a) a chamber(s) as an integral part(s) of or permanently aligned with the bore(s) and (b) a short stock designed to be gripped by one hand and at an angle to and extending below the line of the bore(s). Refer to Figure 1.4, which depicts a modern pistol.

**Figure 2.6** The Ruger AC-556 is a select-fire version of the Ruger Mini-14 rifle. The selector switch is located on the right side of the receiver and offers single shot, three-round burst, or fully automatic operation (Image from author's collection).

**Figure 2.7** A firearm suppressor that is partially disassembled showing the contained Nielson device and end cap (Image from author's collection).

Revolver: A projectile weapon of the pistol type that has a breechloading, chambered cylinder that is arranged in such a way that the cocking of the hammer or movement of the trigger rotates it and brings the next cartridge in line with the barrel for firing. See the revolver in Figure 2.8.

# Regulated and Non-Regulated Manufacturing

**Figure 2.8** Smith and Wesson Model 1917 revolver with lanyard. This veteran of the war to end all wars, World War I, displays the classic lines of a revolver (Image from author's collection).

Rifle: A weapon designed or redesigned, made or remade, and intended to be fired from the shoulder and designed or redesigned and made or remade to use the energy of the explosive in a fixed cartridge to fire only a single projectile through a rifled bore for each single pull of the trigger and shall include any such weapon that may be readily restored to fire a fixed cartridge.

Weapon Made from a Rifle: (a) A rifle having a barrel or barrels of less than 16 inches in length and (b) a weapon made from a rifle if such weapon, as modified, has an overall length of less than 26 inches or a barrel or barrels of less than 16 inches in length. Refer to Figure 2.2 for an example of a rifle.

Shotgun: A weapon designed or redesigned, made or remade, and intended to be fired from the shoulder and designed or redesigned and made or remade to use the energy of the explosive in a fixed shotgun shell to fire through a smooth bore either a number of projectiles (ball shot) or a single projectile for each pull of the trigger and shall include any such weapon that may be readily restored to fire a fixed shotgun shell.

Weapon Made from a Shotgun: (a) A shotgun having a barrel or barrels of less than 18 inches in length and (b) a weapon made from a shotgun if such weapon, as modified, has an overall length of less than 26 inches or a barrel or barrels of less than 18 inches in length.

In addition, "other" and "pistol-grip firearm"[28] are also classification types. Both designations are used to describe the firearm type on a retail firearm transactions record form. Refer to Figure 1.6 for an example of the "other" type of firearm. Figure 2.9 depicts a pistol-grip shotgun, which is distinct from a shotgun, as described, because of the presence of a pistol-style

**Figure 2.9** Mossberg 930SPX pistol-grip shotgun. The same model is available with a standard style stock as well (Image courtesy of O.F. Mossberg & Sons, Inc.).

grip rather than a more traditional style stock, such as the one shown in the rifle depicted in Figure 2.2.

## Self-Manufacture of a Regulated Firearm

Up to this point, this text has focused on private individuals as a non-licensed, non-regulated entity manufacturing their own non-regulated firearms. However, in the United States, the non-licensed individual may also manufacture a *regulated* firearm if the project, as a proposed article, is properly registered and the appropriate tax is paid to the ATF. Regulated firearms include machine guns,[29] short-barreled rifles or shotguns, destructive devices, suppressors, and "any other weapons." In order to lawfully manufacture a regulated firearm, the builder must file ATF Form 1 (*Application to Make and Register a Firearm*), describing the proposed firearm and providing certain identifying and contact information. The instrument is submitted with fingerprints, a photograph of the registrant, and payment for the proper amount of excise tax on the device.[30] When the build is approved, the applicant/registrant receives the document with a canceled "tax stamp" affixed that shows tax has been paid, and the registration is approved. The registrant then engraves the receiver of their firearm with the requisite information as filed, i.e., manufacturer name, manufacturer's location (city and state using recognized abbreviations), serial and model number, and caliber. If the firearm was "remade" from an existing firearm receiver, expect to see two different manufacturers' identities conspicuously engraved on the receiver[31] – the original and the remanufacturer.

The term *manufacture* is used somewhat loosely, here, as there may not be any actual fabrication that takes place. Rather, manufacture or manufacturing encompasses the process of simply "making" the regulated firearm by whichever means and methods are required to do so – whether it is by merely removing and replacing parts or actually involves cutting, trimming, or other types of more complex labors. Consider several examples

# Regulated and Non-Regulated Manufacturing

– if one wanted to manufacture a short-barreled shotgun, he or she would merely cut the barrel down to less than 16" while maintaining an overall length of 26" or more. A shotgun barrel can be cut down in a matter of minutes using a hack saw or even a pipe cutter. However, if a shorter barrel were available through commercial channels, merely installing said short barrel on the receiver would constitute a "manufacturing" or "making" event.

According to 2020 ATF statistics, during 2019, 28,600 Form 1 applications were filed, indicating this many proposals to self-manufacture a regulated firearm or remake a firearm into a regulated firearm. There is no statistic given to the number of approvals or denials, but it is likely that the vast majority were approved, and tax was collected. It is likely that many, if not most, of these proposals did not involve any manufacturing in the true sense of the word but merely required the installation of a barrel or other component that may have required only basic tools. By comparison, there were 170,182 Form 4[32] applications filed. As is the case with the Form 1 filings, the number of approvals and disapprovals of these applications is not given, but it can be reasonably surmised that the majority of applicants were qualified and approved because it seems unlikely that a prohibited person would go through the expense and effort only to be turned away and face possible legal consequences. Between 2014 and 2019, nearly 200,000 Form 1 applications were filed. The number of applications peaked in 2016 and has steadily declined into 2019. Form 4 activity peaked in 2017, fell off sharply in 2018, but had almost returned to 2017 levels by 2019. Figure 2.10 demonstrates the trends in Form 1 and Form 4 applications. As of April 2020, the ATF reported 6,634,064 registered firearms of all types cataloged within the National Firearms Registration and Transfer Record (NFRTR).

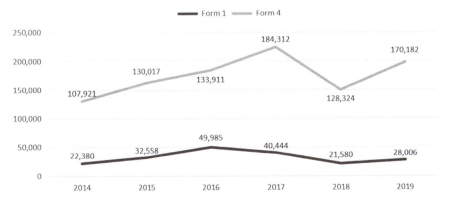

**Figure 2.10** Form 1 & Form 4 applications by year 2014–2019.

## Notes

1. It is unlawful for any person to produce a firearm as proscribed in 18 U.S.C. 922(p).
   "It shall be unlawful for any person to manufacture, import, sell, ship, deliver, possess, transfer, or receive any firearm—
   (A) that, after removal of grips, stocks, and magazines, is not as detectable as the Security Exemplar, by walk-through metal detectors calibrated and operated to detect the Security Exemplar; or
   (B) any major component of which, when subjected to inspection by the types of x-ray machines commonly used at airports, does not generate an image that accurately depicts the shape of the component. Barium sulfate or other compounds may be used in the fabrication of the component."
2. Some states do require the affixing of identifying information onto a receiver by a permanent means. ATF proposed rules under ATF2021R-05 change this and specify a "PMF"or privately made firearm must be affixed with a unique serial number by a licensee, such as a gunsmith.
3. See 18 U.S.C. 922(a) and 923(a); 27 CFR 478.41.
4. Case number 8:14-cr-00167-JVS
5. U.S. Attorney's Annual Statistical Report Fiscal Year 2019, Table 3C, page 15: 93% of defendants charged under 18 U.S.C. § 922 or 924 were found guilty of firearms or other offense.
6. This identification of a firearm receiver is found within regulatory language 27 CFR Part § 478.11.
7. The AR-15 is not the only firearm that uses a bifurcated receiver design. ATF Ruling 2008-1 reclassified the "receiver" of an FN-FNC rifle from the lower receiver to the upper receiver. This ruling encompassed the FN-FAL and the FN-SCAR as well and placed caveats on model designations on similar future rifle designs that may mimic the FN-FNC. It is worth noting that this is inconsistent with the application of language of defining characteristics of a receiver in light of the Roh argument. The proposed rulemaking under ATF 2021R-05 amends the existing language defining a frame or receiver more broadly which would encompass such a design.
8. YouTube video, "Illegal Firearm Maker 'Dr. Death' Helped Create Untraceable 'Ghost Guns.'" Federal authorities are concerned about dangerous, untraceable firearms known as "ghost guns" being illicitly produced in machine shops without licenses or background checks. Juliette Goodrich reports (May 16, 2016).
9. In June, 2021 H.R. 4225, "3d Printed Gun Safety Act of 2021" was introduced in the U.S. House of Representatives. The following month a similar measure was introduced in the U.S. Senate, S.2319. Both bills seek to criminalize the publishing of plans to create firearms using 3D printers.
10. The ATF reports that during 2019, 3,986,663 were imported, a slight decline from the 2018 number. The year 2018 is used in the text for continuity with the other 2018 figures.
11. is the earliest year on record.
12. Ruger manufactures all types of firearms, but only rifles are used here for the sake of contrast between a large company and a small enterprise.

13. A Type 7 SOT holder but mainly known as the preeminent specialist in AK pattern firearms in the United States.
14. The National Instant Criminal Background System is a web-based portal through which licensed retail firearms dealers submit prospective purchasers identifying information. A firearm cannot be delivered to the customer without an approval. Regardless, a waiting period may still apply before the firearm can be delivered to the customer. This background check is required by Public Law 103-159.
15. The last four U.S. general elections have all seen spikes in gun sales.
16. This forecast makes two assumptions. The first is a single firearm is sold per NICS background check. If multiple firearms are purchased simultaneously by the same buyer in the same transaction, a single background check is run. The second is that there would actually be 52,000,000 (51,720,000 to be more precise) firearms available to be sold on the market. Other confounding variables to the NICS reporting are private sales in which a background check is run, therefore, the firearm already exists and could not be counted as a newly manufactured firearm. NICS background checks are also made for non-sale situations such as guns returned to an owner from pawn shops, law enforcement agencies, and even for gun rentals in some venues. Therefore, this projection is a hypothetical figure.
17. In November 2020, a lawsuit was filed in the U.S. District Court for the Southern District of California challenging the legality of the California Department of Justice roster of approved handguns. In essence, the suit seeks relief because certain firearms that are not legal for sale in California are perfectly legal and commercially sold in other states (*Renna v. Becerra*).
18. 3:20-cv-06761. An interesting confederation of plaintiffs including the State of California, an anti-gun special interest group, and two private citizens.
19. The lawsuit cites at least 19 instances involving the seizure of one or more ghost guns. While not expressly stated in the language of the lawsuit, in each one of these cited examples, there is concurrent or underlying criminal activities afoot, i.e., bank robbery, narcotics trade, possession of a firearm by a prohibited person, and human trafficking to name a few. In each instance, possession and/or use of firearms would already be unlawful under existing laws completely absent the ghost gun angle.
20. Case No. 1:20-CV-06885-GHW in the U.S. District Court Southern District of New York. Other plaintiffs are San Jose, CA, Chicago, IL, Columbia, SC, Everytown for Gun Safety Action Fund, and Everytown for Gun Safety Support Fund. The Court subsequently denied the motion, and the matter is pending appeal.
21. PA 19-6—sHB 7219 An Act Concerning Ghost Guns.
22. The State of Washington filed a similar case in July 2018, which was joined by several other state attorneys.
23. According to Justia, the District of Columbia, the commonwealths of Massachusetts and Pennsylvania, and the states of Maryland, Washington, New York, Connecticut, New Jersey, Oregon, North Carolina, Minnesota, Vermont, Colorado, Illinois, Iowa, Virginia, Rhode Island, Delaware, Hawaii, and California are named as plaintiffs. In addition to Defense Distributed, the suit names the Directorate of Defense Trade Controls, U.S. Department

of State, Sarah Heidema, Second Amendment Foundation, Inc, Michael R. Pompeo, Conn Williamson, Mike Miller and Second Amendment Foundation, Inc. as defendants. See https://dockets.justia.com/docket/washington/wawdce/2:2018cv01115/262717.
24. The following terms are taken from 27 CFR Part §479.11 as published on the ATF website.
25. Arguments from Case 91-164 presented January 13, 1992. Many considered the decision against the government to be a benchmark, as the government seldomly loses firearms cases. Recall earlier in this chapter where United States Attorney's claim a 92% conviction rate.
26. Ruling 2011-4.
27. The bump stock was banned by the Trump administration in March 2019 through regulatory process; see the Federal Register Volume 83, No. 246, published Wednesday, December 26, 2018. Prior to this action, critics of the National Rifle Association (NRA) claimed the organization was somehow colluding, lobbying, influencing, or otherwise coordinating with the Trump administration to not take action on the bump stock. The NRA appears to have waffled on the topic with conflicting statements, leaving many to wonder what the organization's position actually was. By the time the federal regulation went into effect, many states had already banned the devices. Ironically, prior to this regulatory action, the bump stock and similar devices had already been subjected to numerous evaluations that deemed the devices a non-regulated gun part. Opponents to the ban cited concerns over a slippery slope precedent which opened the door to simply allow executive orders to supercede due process.
28. See the Firearms Transaction Record, Form 4473, page 6 under Section D, types – firearms that are neither handguns nor long guns (rifles or shotguns), such as firearms having a pistol grip that expel a shotgun shell (pistol-grip firearm).
29. There is currently no provision to make a machine gun except for governmental use or export.
30. The excise tax is $200 for a machine gun, suppressor, destructive devices, and short-barreled rifles/shotguns. "Any other weapons" require a $5 payment. These amounts were established in 1934 and remain unchanged. Using the U.S. Bureau of Labor Statistics CPI calculator (https://www.bls.gov/data/inflation_calculator.htm), $200 in January 1934 would be equivalent to $4,136.41 in July 2021. A $5 bill in January 1934 would be equivalent to $103.41.
31. For example, a rifle that someone wants to remake into a short-barreled rifle would require a Form 1 to be submitted and approved. Because this involved remaking from a pre-existing receiver, secondary maker markings would be engraved to reflect who remade the rifle into a short-barreled rifle. See Figure 2.6.
32. The Form 4 is a tax-paid application to transfer an NFA firearm between parties. The transfer must be approved by the ATF, and the appropriate tax paid before the transaction takes place.

# References

ATF. (2015, January 2). ATF. Retrieved July 4, 2020, from *Manufacturing and Gunsmithing*: https://www.atf.gov/firearms/docs/ruling/2015-1-manufacturing-and-gunsmithing

ATF. (2017, November 6). Firearms. Retrieved March 2020, from *ATF.gov*: https://www.atf.gov/firearms/qa/does-individual-need-license-make-firearm-personal-use

ATF. (2019, November 8). Regulations. Retrieved July 4, 2020, from *ATF*: https://regulations.atf.gov/478-11/2016-12100#478-11-p2068244760

ATF. (2019). Reports. Retrieved March 2020, from *ATF*: https://www.atf.gov/firearms/docs/report/2019-firearms-commerce-report/download

ATF. (2020). ATF.gov. Retrieved March 2021, from *Resources*: https://www.atf.gov/firearms/docs/report/firearmscommercereport2020pdf/download

ATF. (2021). *Definition of "Frame or Receiver" and Identification of Firearms*.

Blumenthal, R., et al. (2018, July 31). United States Congress. Retrieved May 15, 2020, from *115th Congress Legislation*: https://www.congress.gov/bill/115th-congress/senate-bill/3300/text?q=%7B%22search%22%3A%5B%22ghost+gun%22%5D%7D&r=3&s=5

Brady Campaign to Prevent Gun Violence. (2018, December 19). *Brady v State Department*. Retrieved April 11, 2020, from *Brady Campaign to Prevent Gun Violence*: https://www.bradyunited.org/legal-case/brady-v-state-department

Complaint for Declaratory and Injunctive Relief, 3:20-cv-06761 (United States District Court Northern District of California September 29, 2020).

Department of Justice. (2014, October 2). Press Releases, 14–133. Retrieved July 4, 2020, from *ATF.gov*: https://www.atf.gov/news/pr/owner-la-habra-manufacturing-firm-charged-illegally-manufacturing-and-selling-key-0

FBI. (2020, August 31). NICS Background Checks: Month/Year. Retrieved September 12, 2020, from *fbi.gov*: https://www.fbi.gov/file-repository/nics_firearm_checks_-_month_year.pdf/view

Hagstrom, A. (2020, July 1). Gun Sales in 2020 Are Absolutely Crushing Records. Retrieved July 26, 2020, from *The Daily Caller* https://dailycaller.com/2020/07/01/2020-gun-sales-june-record-fbi/

Levine, P., & McKnight, R. (2020, July 13). UP FRONT Three Million More Guns: The Spring 2020 Spike in Firearm Sales. Retrieved July 26, 2020, from *Brookings Institute*: https://www.brookings.edu/blog/up-front/2020/07/13/three-million-more-guns-the-spring-2020-spike-in-firearm-sales/

Smith, A. (2021, February 1). More Guns Than Ever Sold during Month of Capitol Riot, FBI Background Checks Suggest Retrieved March 9, 2021, from *Forbes*: https://www.forbes.com/sites/aaronsmith/2021/02/01/more-guns-than-ever-sold-during-month-of-capitol-riots-according-to-fbi-background-checks/?sh=d462836377a6

# The Frame, Firearm Components, and Firearm Accessories

# 3

> Firearm frame or receiver. That part of a firearm which provides housing for the hammer, bolt or breechblock, and firing mechanism, and which is usually threaded at its forward portion to receive the barrel.
>
> (United States Code)

Under rulemaking authority the ATF seeks to redefine the meanings of the terms firearm frame or receiver which expands the definition beyond the basic scope quoted here.

> "The new definition more broadly describes a 'frame or receiver' as one that provides housing or a structure designed to hold or integrate any fire control component. Unlike the prior definitions of 'frame or receiver' that were rigidly tied to three specific fire control components (i.e., those necessary for the firearm to initiate or complete the firing sequence), the new regulatory definition is intended to be general enough to encompass changes in technology and parts terminology"
>
> **(ATF, 2021).**

## Crossing the Threshold: Is It a Receiver or a Blank?

So, when does a firearm become a firearm? The question seems rhetorical. When does something become something else? When is the transformation complete? When does an object transcend the plane of the basic building block or fundamental matter or materials into a defined and recognized iteration? This point was pondered in a popular television sitcom in which the main characters were forced to confront the difficult question: When did a pizza became a pizza? Was it a pizza when it went into the oven, or was it a pizza only when it was removed from the oven after baking? All constructed articles require the investment of labor and the combination of materials to go from disjointed parts into a sum whole and completed, finished item. What and where, then, should be the threshold at which basic material becomes a firearm frame or receiver? Although the slide is removed, the frame in Figure 3.1 is present and would still be definable as a firearm, as the frame is in a state in which it is readily restored to function. In fact, reassembling the pistol in Figure 3.1 would take mere moments. The frame in Figure 3.1 was well beyond the *critical state* of manufacture, "when the article becomes sufficiently complete to function as a frame or receiver, or may readily be completed, assembled, converted, or restored to accept the parts it is intended to house or hold" (ATF, 2021). All one would need to do is replace the slide back onto the frame and insert a loaded magazine; therefore, it is reasonable to deem the frame as depicted in Figure 3.1 as a functional firearm, even absent the presence of the slide, due to the ease and speed which it could be reassembled into a fully operating firearm. The receiver or frame serves as the basis or core to which parts are assembled onto to make the firearm wholly assembled and ready to function. So, if the receiver is unavailable or absent, one simply cannot assemble a firearm; they are left with a loose assortment of parts from which a final assembly cannot take place. Contrast Figure 3.1 and Figure 3.2 and note the differences. Although certain milling processes have been done to the receiver in Figure 3.2, it has still not progressed to the point where all parts could be assembled together to complete the build. Nonetheless, within the language of ATF 2021R-05, which proposes to refine the current definition of the term "frame or receiver", the partially completed workpiece depicted in Figure 3.2 would be considered a "firearm" because

**Figure 3.1** The frame of a Walther PP. The grips are removed, showing the internal mechanisms. The barrel is integrated to the frame, and the recoil spring surrounds the barrel, contributing to the compactness of the pistol's clean lines (Image from author's collection).

# Frame, Components, and Accessories

**Figure 3.2** A partially completed pistol frame complete with the jig fixture. (Image by Phil Puglisi; used with permission).

it is part of a "weapons parts kit" (note the jig present in the frame) which provides the materials and means to construct a firearm in a "short period of time with minimal effort". The proposed guidance, as part of the expanded meanings of the terms frame or receiver also considers a "partially complete, disassembled, or inoperable frame or receiver".

Prior to releasing ATF 2021R-05, the ATF had published a series of guidance communicating the determinations which had been made by their own Firearms Technology Branch, which had reviewed various sample "receiver blanks". Consider several predicate examples:

> Receiver blanks that do not meet the definition of a "firearm" are not subject to regulation under the Gun Control Act (GCA). ATF has long held that items such as receiver blanks, "castings" or "machined bodies" in which the fire-control cavity area is completely solid and un-machined have not reached the "stage of manufacture" which would result in the classification of a firearm according to the GCA.
>
> (ATF, 2020)

So far as the AR-type lower receiver is concerned, the lack of the cavities for the fire control parts to be installed, lack of pin holes in the sidewalls by which to install a hammer and trigger, as well as other features within the receiver are irrelevant when contemplated against the new interpretations of a firearm frame or receiver. The proposed rulemaking changes specifically directly address the "split receiver" configuration to bring the "lower" portion into the meaning of a frame or receiver. The new rules also ensure that, even in an incomplete stage of manufacture and absent internal components, such an item would still be definable as a receiver. The raw forging depicted in Figure 5.3 (bottom exemplar) exemplifies this criteria under proposed meaning four of a frame or receiver. Figures 5.3, 5.4, and 5.5 in Chapter 5 of this text further illustrate these points.

Chapter 1 of this text cites correspondence between the ATF FTISB (Firearms Technology Industry Services Branch) and an attorney representing Polymer80 Incorporated. In the correspondence, openly published on the Polymer80 website, the submitted sample AR-10 type receiver blank was deemed a "non-gun," as it was "not sufficiently complete to be classified as the frame or receiver of a firearm" (ATF, 2020). When referring back to the metrics published on the ATF website, the reasoning is consistent, as the submitted sample was "completely solid and un-machined in the fire-control recess area" (ATF, 2020). However, added details appear, stating that "the most forward portion of the rear takedown pin lug clearance area measures approximately 1.32 inches in length, less than the maximum allowable 1.60-inch threshold" (ATF, 2020). There were 11 features noted as present by the examiner, and five were either not complete or present.[1] Also noted in the report was the absence of any indicators or markings to aid or guide in making the receiver, a point not mentioned in the online reference. With respect to the Polymer80 "CG" or "CG9" submitted sample, the FTSIB used a Glock 17 handgun frame/receiver as a comparison piece. As was the case with the Polymer80 AR-10-type lower receiver blank, the CG and CG9 were not determined to be firearms.

The origin of the term *80% receiver* is not entirely clear, nor is it clear how this percentage was calculated or why 80% makes a good threshold. Mathematically it makes little sense because anything over .50, fifty, or halves is considered a majority/minority statement. In general manufacturing terms, the work or effort invested in creating an item using any production methods (CNC cutting, chemical milling, additive manufacturing methods, etc.) is generally measured by the amount of time and/or the number of operations required to transform the basic material into the final product.[2] The ATF did not use terms such as "80% receiver", "80% finished", "80% complete", and "unfinished receiver" to define a workpiece in progress which had yet met the stage of completion to be defined as a functional frame or receiver. These terms are colloquial in nature but have gained a general acceptance to meaning in the firearms community.

Frame, Components, and Accessories 51

Perhaps some context into the 80% question can be gleaned from *State of California et al. v. ATF et al.* On Page 29 of the plaintiff's complaint, three examples are cited that characterize the time frame to transform the non-receiver workpiece into a receiver as the primary factor in determining how far along the state of readiness and assemblage the workpiece is before it becomes a definable firearm. The plaintiff cites three communications encompassing three different receiver determinations made for three different members of the industry by three different ATF officials.[3] In each of these examples, the proposed samples[4] were all deemed firearms because it took some 75 minutes to transform the article into what was deemed a functional firearm receiver. The time determination, however, is elastic. In fact, in the third cited exhibit, the investment of time is predicated upon two assumptions: a "competent individual" and "having the necessary equipment." The proposed expanded meaning of a frame or receiver to include a "weapons parts kit" effectively negates the stage of manufacture argument. The ATF has a mandate to provide objective and true guidance to the industries they serve; therefore, a definitive line must be established to segregate a firearm and a non-firearm, at least as the current verbiage suggests, "critical stage of manufacture".

The 2021R-05 proposal, as well as other recent rule change proposals, and ruling reversals published by the ATF may very well go into effect; however, it is very likely, if not evitable, these proposals are going to be litigated in the courts. In the meanwhile, the status of the affected articles will be in limbo.

## Functional versus Operable

In the author's professional experience as an investigator and firearms examiner, the question of a *functional* versus *operable* firearm frequently arose. To successfully prosecute a firearms case, there must be evidence offered to the court that the exhibit in question is a firearm; therefore, the exhibit must meet the legal definition of the same. If testimony is not offered that proves that the offered case evidence is a firearm, the charges are going to dissipate because the lack of evidence renders the state unable to prove the elements of the crime alleged. Commonly, this testimony is rendered by a credentialed expert who articulates how the evidence exhibit meets the legal definition of a firearm. To meet the burden of proof, the witness had to testify the exhibit was functional. The standard practice was that the examiner would conduct a safety and functional examination and test fire the exhibit, which would verify its function. The examiner would publish a report stating the facts and findings of the analysis. If the evidence exhibit chambered and fired ammunition, this was all that was required. Even if the exhibit only fired once, or even if the complete cycle of operation did not occur because of mechanical failure, maintenance issue, or other inhibiting condition, it could be said the exhibit still functioned as a firearm, capable of expelling a projectile under the force of an explosive.

The author is familiar with a case in which firearms were seized during the execution of a search warrant at a private residence. Although firearms were not specifically articulated in the warrant and were outside the scope of the original investigation which provided the probable cause for the warrant to be issued, several firearms turned up during the search, at least two of the located firearms were suspicious enough to merit further investigation. One receiver, while not wholly assembled into a complete firearm, was deemed by a credentialled expert a functional receiver and declared contraband by virtue of its design features. The other was also illegally configured.

Suppose the exhibit under study is found to be inoperable. A firearm may be inoperable, yet it may still be considered functional. Consider this parallel: a motor vehicle that has run out of fuel or has suffered a flat tire or some other repairable circumstance is still a motor vehicle; although in its present state it is not operable; it remains a functional motor vehicle. If the condition is remedied by putting fuel in the vehicle, changing the tire, or fixing the breakdown, the vehicle is restored to full operation. Firearms, as mechanical devices, can and do incur failures that might prevent operation but do not in any way impede function. The proper function of a firearm may be affected by any number of variables that the experienced, credentialed subject matter expert is cognizant of, whereas the layperson may not be. For the sake of illustration, consider a hypothetical, yet very plausible, scenario: a layperson attempts to perform a test fire to determine whether the exhibit, suspected to be a firearm, will actually discharge a projectile under the force of an explosive. This individual is unable to make the firearm discharge and opines that the exhibit is not a functional firearm. As presented, what bearing would this have on a case in which the burden of proof lies in proving the evidence is a functional firearm? Obviously, this could cause the case to be dropped, even though it is entirely possible that a credentialed subject matter expert could recognize an issue that prevented the exhibit from operating. Common issues include:

- Ammunition issues; defective cartridge or improper caliber.
- Lack of or improper maintenance, resulting in a temporary, easily remedied restoration.
- Mechanical failure caused by a broken or worn component or improper reassembly.
- Lack of familiarity on the part of the layperson examiner to the object under study.

In this offered hypothetical illustration, the individual is not properly credentialed to undertake a firearms examination because they have forsaken the presence of a functional receiver and confused it with a question of operability, let alone what is affecting the operation of the study subject. If such examinations were undertaken by under or non-credentialled persons and there is an erroneous conclusion made by such persons, this could create potential impediments to the case or, at the very least, embarrassment.

The examiner must disclose any issues with function that are discovered and what, if any, actions were required to actually make the firearm discharge to discern an inoperable versus a non-functioning firearm. The examiner could make a repair and attempt a test fire. Any of these discoveries or actions should be documented on the examiner's report. If there is an intention to submit the firearm evidence to IBIS/NIBIN (Integrated Ballistic Identification System/National Integrated Ballistic Information Network), any repairs that would cause changes to individual characteristics must be disclosed to prevent a misidentification.

Within the communities of crime labs that work firearms cases, it is a common lab practice to retain exemplar firearms and parts to form a reference library. One stated purpose of such a library would be to allow an examiner access to firearms parts and conduct further testing if a part is discovered to be broken, or the exhibit, say in the case of a striped receiver, is completely devoid of parts and, therefore, a complete build would be required to affirm the receiver could be completed into an operable firearm. The author recalls a specific instance in which a privately made firearm was uncovered as part of a broader, non-firearm focused, investigation. Although the receiver and barrel were mated, there were no internal parts installed including the bolt and fire control parts. An outside lab offered to loan the author the missing internal parts so that the completed exhibit could be fully assembled and tested. In this case, it turned out to be unnecessary. Nonetheless, having access to such parts is invaluable when the need arises. In furtherance of this effort, the working firearms examiner should have access to the most detailed schematics and plans for any firearm for just such a contingency. Not only is it important to articulate the proper name or identify a certain part, should loaner parts be necessary, the examiner should be able to articulate them by proper nomenclature.

Any of the aforementioned issues are temporary conditions that are easily rectified. If the inhibiting condition is temporary and easily fixed, this meets the plain English meaning of the verbiage, "readily restored to function." A broken firing pin may prevent a firearm from discharging a round of ammunition when the trigger is pressed; nevertheless, replacing the firing pin in many firearms is a job that takes a few minutes. Even if faced with such conditions, insomuch as the frame or receiver is present, the examiner could still affirm that the exhibit under study is a firearm.

## Safety Considerations

Test firing firearms can be a daunting task fraught with danger to the examiner. Oftentimes, evidence firearms come in with unknown conditions that affect their safe function. This statement includes both professionally manufactured and privately made firearms. A professionally made firearm by a recognized name plate manufacturer may have been subjected to modifications and alterations, aftermarket, non-spec parts of unknown quality, as well as other "mischiefs" by persons with limited to no knowledge of actual firearm mechanics. Often, these "jail breaks," as they are commonly called, or alterations and modifications are focused on enhancing or improving firearm function or creating other behaviors, such as converting a semi-automatic firearm and making it capable of fully automatic fire. The privately made firearm is suspectable to all of the above with an added dimension: it is unclear how well the receiver was fabricated. An undereducated or ill-informed builder may install parts suitable for an airsoft gun but would not be suitable to handle the stresses of a real firearm. The receiver could have been out of specification – receiver walls too thin, pin holes out of place, a barrel only hand threaded on and not properly torqued to specification, or other critical dimensions ignored. To compound this problem, fabricators sometimes attempt to correct mistakes by soldering or welding material onto the workpiece. The author is familiar with damaged receiver blanks being repaired using a high-strength adhesive. All create unknown hazards.

To counter safety concerns, many labs have gun benches or rests in which the exhibit is secured, bore pointed to the bullet trap, and the trigger is pressed remotely allowing the examiner to stand a distance away. Whatever safety measures are in place, nothing replaces the experienced and knowledgeable examiner on the bench who could recognize potential issues beforehand while making a pre-exam safety inspection. The author, as an examiner who worked actual casework, never had an issue with a firearm and this is attributed to knowledge and diligence.

## Non-Guns

There are conditions that arise in which a submitted exhibit will not and cannot meet the definition of a firearm. *Non-guns* are just that: *non-guns*. Figure 3.3 depicts a model gun that could easily deceive the casual viewer into believing it is a real firearm. A non-gun *may appear* to be a firearm but, in fact, is not capable of function nor is it readily restored to function; in fact, it is it completely inert and serves no useful purpose as a firearm.

Frame, Components, and Accessories 55

**Figure 3.3** At first glance, many people would mistake this as an actual Model 1928 Thompson Submachine gun. In fact, it is a completely inert, commercially manufactured model. It is constructed of wood and metal components (Image by Phil Puglisi; used with permission).

It is common practice to create dummy guns, analogs, or props by taking inert dummy non-gun receivers and joining them with authentic components. These items are used for theatrical purposes, display, training, or other endeavors for which the appearance of a firearm is desired without concern for safety or legalities.

Consider the DEWAT, short for deactivated war trophy. A DEWAT is created by rendering the receiver useless by cutting or other destructive means, yet preserves the remaining components, especially the barrel and stock, to preserve the look. The prescribed method for destroying a receiver has evolved over the years. At one time, merely plugging the barrel, grinding off a firing pin, or stripping the receiver of internal parts to render it inoperable yet still functional were acceptable practices, but this is no longer the case and would not meet the requirements to be considered a DEWAT. Under new proposed definitions for a receiver, even a destroyed receiver is defined, "The term 'frame or receiver' shall not include a frame or receiver that is destroyed. For purposes of this definition, the term 'destroyed' means that the frame or receiver has been permanently altered not to provide housing or a structure that may hold or integrate any fire control or essential internal component, and may not readily be assembled, completed, converted, or restored to a functional state. Acceptable methods of destruction include completely melting, crushing, or shredding the frame or receiver, or by completely severing at least three critical areas of the frame or receiver using a cutting torch having a tip of sufficient size to displace at least 1/4 inch of material at each location." (ATF, 2021).

Other devices such as airsoft guns, paint ball guns (identified as paintball *markers* in some venues to avoid the use of the term *gun*), line throwing devices, harpoon or spear guns, power actuated tools (PATs), and flare guns are not considered firearms within the context of their ordinary use unless converted to function as a firearm. This in no way implies any of these articles could not be defined as a dangerous weapon if used with malicious intent to commit an assault. In such instances, a properly credentialled, competent, and experienced firearms examiner should be consulted to make a determination as to whether the item could be deemed a dangerous weapon.

The author was tasked with a case that involved the use of a non-gun in the commission of a crime. The exhibit was, at one time, a factory made semi-automatic pistol. At some point the *prop* had been rendered useless by removing all the internal components, cutting the frame, and deforming the barrel. The receiver had been cut in such a way to prevent the pistol slide from attaching to the frame. All of which had rendered the prop inert and incapable of being restored to function. The prop was recovered from a suspect who had just committed a robbery at a convenience store. The evidence was declared non-functional and testimony to that effect was offered before the court. There was no way this prop was functional at the time of seizure, nor, at least in the author's opinion, was there any way it was readily restored to function. Although the cashier believed the subject was armed with a gun, and, in fact, the presented prop used to facilitate the robbery was, at one time, an actual firearm, these points do not necessarily guarantee a conviction for robbery with a firearm.

If the submitted exhibit suspected of being a firearm consists only of a receiver and is incomplete as a whole firearm. If the evidence is riding on a receiver or non-receiver determination, the expert must consider if the workpiece has surpassed the "critical stage of manufacture" using whichever definitions are in place and how court rulings will interpret those rule changes when legal challenges are brought. One major point likely to be argued would be the "grandfathered" status of any pre-existing articles which were not regulated but later became regulated. Traditionally, such items were allowed since it was expected their numbers would decline thru attrition as time went on and they would be relegated to a less circulated status. Grandfathered status has been a tricky issue historically with items which were made absent any identifiers, such as a serial number, which can be used to determine a production date. ATF 2021R-05 dispenses with any "grandfathering" argument by claiming it is impractical to discern if a receiver blank was made before a certain date.

Frame, Components, and Accessories

## Components, Parts, and Accessories

There are firearm components that are not frames or receivers but are either regulated or prohibited either at the state or federal level or both. Gun stocks were not ordinarily regulated, however even this has changed. In the instance of the bump stock the device was banned by regulatory edict.[5] Some states had already independently banned the bump stock and some triggers that mimicked fully automatic fire in advance of Federal action. "Included within the definition of machinegun is any part designed and intended solely and exclusively, or combination of parts designed and intended, for use in converting a weapon into a machinegun" (ATF, 2009). The components under discussion in this passage include the drop in auto sear (DIAS), Lightning Link, as well as certain other sears and trigger packs for various firearms.[6] Recall the discussion in Chapter 2 of the arraignment of Davud Sungur, who was accused of 3D-printing a device similar in function, if not appearance, to the drop in auto sear shown in Figure 3.4.

A firearm accessory is anything that is added to the firearm, but its presence is not required for the firearm to function or operate. An accessory could be an aesthetic adornment or provide some benefit to the shooter.

**Figure 3.4** The drop in auto sear is not permanently installed in a lower receiver, allowing it to be transferred from one host gun to another (Image from author's collection).

## Non-Regulated Components

The balance of parts required to assemble a wholly made and operable firearm are considered *non-regulated* parts or accessories. Historically parts and accessories were, with some minor exceptions, non-regulated items; however, this longstanding practice is shifting also. Accessories have retroactively subjected to controls. Firearm parts, on the other hand, are dedicated to completing firearms assembly, including barrels, stocks and grips, trigger and fire-control components, magazine wells, revolver cylinders, and scope mounts and bases. These parts are those that are brought together and joined to a functional frame/receiver that render a firearm operable. Figure 3.5 depicts small parts for a handgun and could be used to assemble a new firearm or repair or upgrade an existing one. Figure 3.6 is a barrel and Figure 3.7 is a pistol slide with a reflex style optic installed. The items presented in Figures 3.5, 3.6, and 3.7 are all unregulated components that are used to complete a firearm but also to repair, upgrade, or modify an existing firearm. This raises the question: why are these parts not universally regulated like a frame or receiver? There are several answers:

- Non-regulated parts are not used to enable the function of a frame/receiver; they are used to complete the firearm and make it operable

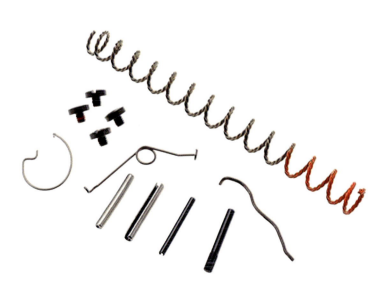

**Figure 3.5** Small internal handgun parts, including assorted springs, pins, and grip screws. There are non-regulated parts (Image courtesy of SIG Sauer).

Frame, Components, and Accessories 59

**Figure 3.6** Barrels are not regulated parts. Some manufacturers do mark a serial number on them to correspond with the frame they were originally attached with (Image courtesy of SIG Sauer).

**Figure 3.7** SIG Sauer P320 pistol slide with a SIG branded reflex optic. Like the small parts in Figure 3.5 and the barrel in Figure 3.6, the slide is not a regulated part. Optics-equipped handguns are becoming more common in the market. The P320 model is modular, meaning it can be configured in different ways for different purposes by swapping "plug and play" components (Image courtesy of SIG Sauer).

but in no way contribute to fashioning or fabricating a new firearm frame or receiver.
- Non-regulated parts are commonly used by gunsmiths, armorers, or private individuals to repair, reconfigure, or improve an existing firearm. Such activities are not deemed to be manufacturing.

- There are legitimate and recognized non-firearm purposes for such parts. For example, barrels, stocks, and accessories are assembled onto a blank or dummy receiver and used as theatrical props, inert training aids, decorations, or displays in museums or other similar venues as previously described.
- The longstanding practice of non-regulated parts may soon be at an end. In July, 2021 Rare Breed Triggers was served with a cease and desist order by the ATF, whom declared the company's "forced reset trigger" a machine gun. The matter is in the opening stages of what will likely result in lengthy litigation. Figure 3.8 depicts the small pieces required to complete the construction of an AR type lower receiver. None of the items depicted in Figure 3.8 are regulated individually or collectively at this time.

**Figure 3.8** AR pattern fire control parts and the other small pieces used to complete the lower receiver. (Image courtesy of CMMG Inc.).

Frame, Components, and Accessories 61

So far as privately made firearms are concerned, what is now being described as *firearm kits* allow builders complete the assembly of their self-made frame or receiver into a completed, operable firearm by acquiring and using professionally made non-regulated firearms parts. These parts are readily available through numerous sources, such as brick and mortar sporting goods shops, gun shops, and even general merchandizers and through catalog sales, telephone orders, and, of course, online.

## Serial Numbered Parts

Privately made firearms may be found with serial numbers or other numbers engraved on parts. In the most likely scenario, parts and accessories that bear serial numbers that may or may not match one another are the product of marrying a parts kit to a different receiver. For vanity purposes, the manufacturer of the receiver could have matched the receiver's own unique serial number to the donor parts kits because a manufacturer enjoys the latitude to mark a serial number of their choosing, as it is a *unique* number to that manufacturer. In the case of a privately made firearm that is not going to be sold or traded, no serial number would appear unless one or more of the following conditions exist:

- The firearm will be transferred or sold.
- State law requires the receiver be marked with a serial number.
- A number is voluntarily affixed by the maker.
- A regulated firearm has been created, i.e., a suppressor, short-barreled rifle, or shotgun, etc.
- If rulemaking changes take effect as articulated in the ATF 2021R-05 proposal the incomplete receiver would require a serial number before being affixed.

It is imperative that only the frame or receiver affixed serial number be used for identification purposes, as this would be the only serial number recorded as part of a transfer or manufacturing record. Serial numbers may appear, either partially or completely, on other parts of the firearm; however, these do not negate the preeminence of the serial number affixed on the frame. Gun parts could be swapped or replaced. This rule also applies to serial numbers not engraved in the receiver but that appear on other parts and are removed or altered in some manner. The gun barrel or pistol slide might be "force matched" to the frame number, and by doing so, the original part's serial number is struck, and the new serial number affixed, but none of this really matters. Some companies, as a matter of routine business practice, will affix serial numbers to all major parts. This practice was once common to many gunmakers but has gradually fallen away, yet some makers do persist with the practice. Serializing the major parts ensures that the gun assembled and tested is the same gun and that all the parts match. It may also provide for accountability of parts inside the factory. Many gunmakers have a multinational presence, and there are venues in which firearm components are more broadly defined than just the frame or receiver, and it may be customary or legally required to affix a serial number to some or all major gun parts.

## Notes

1. In this example, 16 features are articulated by the ATF FTISB; 11 are present, five are absent. Although 80% is the common term, 80% of 16 is 12.8.
2. Arsenal Bulgaria claims it requires 5.5 hours of milling to transform a forged receiver blank into a receiver ready for assembly (https://www.arsenalinc.com/usa/firearms/rifles/sam7-series/).
3. Three different chiefs of the ATF Firearms Technology Branch.
4. An undescribed, partially completed firearm receiver, an AR-15 type receiver, and a 1911-style pistol frame.
5. Federal Register Volume 83, No. 246 published Wednesday, December 26, 2018; Rules and Regulations, Docket No. 2018R–22F; AG Order No. 4367–2018.
6. Historically, many select fire firearms relied on "auto sears" that were required to cause the firearm to perform as a machine gun, capable of firing more than one round per single trigger press; however, as evidenced by examples offered in the text, other devices which are not sears have been reclassified as machine guns and therefore become regulated. Many devices have become regulated or banned although they are not truly auto sears nor cause a firearm to discharge more than a single round per press of the trigger, but instead cause the firearm to fire more quickly by any number of methods including use of recoil to cause the trigger to press more quickly.

## References

ATF. (2009, April). ATF National Firearms Act Handbook. Retrieved July 12, 2020, from *ATF official website*: https://www.atf.gov/file/58251/download

ATF. (2020, April 6). Are "80%" or "Unfinished" Receivers Illegal? Retrieved December 13, 2020, from *Firearms*: https://www.atf.gov/firearms/qa/are-"80"-or-"unfinished"-receivers-illegal

ATF. (2020, February 6). What is an "80%" or "Unfinished" Receiver? Retrieved December 13, 2020, from *Firearms*: https://www.atf.gov/firearms/qa/what-"80"-or-"unfinished-receiver

ATF. (2021). *Definition of "Frame or Receiver" and Identification of Firearms.*

# Fabricating a Receiver and Assembling a Firearm

# 4

The interest in privately made firearms has spawned a new industry of companies that design and supply home builders with jigs, fixtures, parts, supplies, and other suitable tooling and equipment. Both the ease by which privately made firearms can be fabricated and the clearing of the air of misinformation around them has stripped away the most significant impediments to unregulated gun making. Today, one need not have access to industrial machine tools or even have a lot of skill working with materials. Modern technology – computer aided drafting, virtual modeling, and robotics – has created pathways for people to create all kinds of articles inexpensively and easily. Regardless of the specific approach, each makes the building process as simple and foolproof as possible. It is not, however, foolproof and still requires a degree of tool dexterity and competency to properly complete a build. In Chapter 1 of this text, the author referenced an article in *Wired* that discussed three different approaches to constructing a firearm receiver:

1. Three-dimensional (3D) printing or additive manufacturing process
2. Hand and power tools
3. CNC milling machine[1]

Any of these three approaches are shown to be capable of producing a functional final product. Each one could be independently argued on its own merits to have certain advantages over the other. It is worth noting that some types of receivers may be better suited to a certain manufacturing approach over others.

## Additive Manufacturing and 3D Printing

The term "additive manufacturing" references technologies that grow three-dimensional objects one superfine layer at a time. Each successive layer bonds to the preceding layer of melted or partially melted material. It is possible to use different substances for layering material, including metal powder, thermoplastics, ceramics, composites, glass and even edibles like chocolate.

**(GE, 2021)**

DOI: 10.4324/9781003044499-4

The terms additive manufacturing and 3D or three dimensional printing are often used interchangeably because of the similarities between the two manufacturing processes; however, a distinction is drawn – additive manufacturing is used in the context of scaled industrial environments and 3D printing is used for small- or micro-scale projects such as what a hobbyist would produce.[2] 3D printing works in an opposite approach to traditional milling machines: additive manufacturing builds the object up from nothing using whichever media, whereas traditional milling of materials involve cutting and trimming, akin to sculpting, shaping, or carving from rock or wood. Referring to Figure 1.3, the depicted pistol slide shows moderate to heavy "tooling" marks made by the milling machines cutting and shaping the steel blank to form the slide. Figure 4.1 shows a desktop scale 3D printer. The blue polymer material is on the spool and feeds the head, which disperses the production medium to form the object and the platform lowers as the features of the fabricated object are built up. The size of the printer will dictate the limitations of the size of the object that can be fabricated using the machine. Because a firearm frame/receiver is not very large, even modest-size machines that fit on a desktop can accommodate the task.

In addition to fabricating the complete frame or receiver, 3D printing offers home builders the option of fabricating their own small parts, thereby eliminating the need to obtain the non-regulated firearm components from

**Figure 4.1** Justin Yates, an assistant professor at Francis Marion University, teaches the Marines about the capabilities of a 3D printer at Camp Lejeune, N.C., June 2. Additive manufacturing, or 3D printing, allows Marines to produce parts quickly with exact specifications and at almost any location (Image by Cpl. Justin T. Updegraff/; courtesy of U.S. Marine Corps).

Fabricating and Assembling          65

outside sources. This could prove especially beneficial to a builder engaging in research and development of a new or improved concept, such as a firearm mechanism. Figure 4.2 shows a grip fabricated by using additive manufacturing technique and then installed on a Heckler and Koch GLM 40mm grenade launcher. Figure 4.3 shows 3D-printed AR pattern triggers produced at the U.S. Army's Rock Island Arsenal as part of a technology demonstration showing the potential applications in the defense environment. Clearly, such technology is easily capable of allowing the non-regulated individual to craft a firearm or firearm components.

To construct a receiver (or any object for that matter) using a 3D printer, a 3D model is created using software or an application (app). A search of apps and software revealed dozens of third-party programs supported in Windows or iOS environments in addition to original equipment manufacturer software supplied

**Figure 4.2** The grip above was fabricated by using an additive manufacturing technique. As the Army drives toward improving readiness today and modernizing future equipment, the Rock Island Arsenal – Joint Manufacturing and Technology Center (RIA-JMTC) is establishing the foundation to scale additive manufacturing throughout the Army (Image courtesy of the U.S. Army).

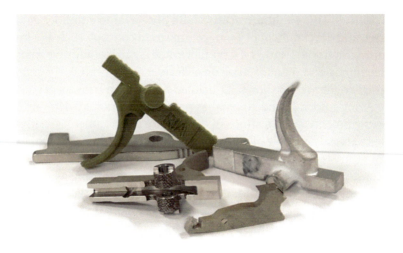

**Figure 4.3** 3D-printed AR pattern triggers. As the Army drives toward improving readiness today and modernizing future equipment, the Rock Island Arsenal – Joint Manufacturing and Technology Center (RIA-JMTC) is establishing the foundation to scale additive manufacturing throughout the Army (Image courtesy of the U.S. Army).

with the purchase of a device. If users are less technically savvy or simply choose to forgo creating their own models, the author was able to locate numerous internet sites hosting design files for firearm frames and receivers. Recall Chapter 1 and the discussion of continuing litigation between Defense Distributed and a collective of individual states' attorneys. This ongoing litigation does not seem to have deterred others from sharing firearm design files across peer-to-peer (p2p), file transfer protocol (FTP), or torrent-type file sharing. Many of these are open source, but some do charge nominal licensing fees to download the pattern. The author located numerous web sites hosting hundreds, if not thousands, of CAD files for suppressors, let alone firearm related small parts or other matter.

If a person constructs a firearm frame or receiver using non-ferrous materials such as polymer, allowances must be made to ensure compliance with the requirements in 18 USC 922(p).

> It shall be unlawful for any person to manufacture, import, sell, ship, deliver, possess, transfer, or receive any firearm—
>
> (A) that, after removal of grips, stocks, and magazines, is not as detectable as the Security Exemplar, by walk-through metal detectors calibrated and operated to detect the Security Exemplar; or

(B) any major component of which, when subjected to inspection by the types of x-ray machines commonly used at airports, does not generate an image that accurately depicts the shape of the component. Barium sulfate or other compounds may be used in the fabrication of the component.

(ATF, 2016)

3D printing represents a significant advancement in materials forming and fabricating with nearly endless uses. Hobbyist-level printers can cost a few hundred dollars and are operated using a smart phone, tablet, or laptop or desktop computer. A modest 3D printer can produce a complete pistol frame in approximately nineteen hours of machine run time. The cost of such a receiver is a few dollars in materials. More complex variants, alongside upgrades to existing equipment allow the machines to weave in various materials, including metals.

## Tools, Jigs, and Fixtures

A second identified approach to fabricating a firearm frame/receiver is using hand and power tools and a jig. It is very likely that this is the most common method of fabricating a frame/receiver because of its relative simplicity and the low cost of acquiring the jigs and fixtures compared to printing or using machine tools. The jigs and fixtures are perpetually reusable so long as they are not damaged. The builder merely has to install the frame/receiver blank into the jig and remove material by drilling and cutting. The jig guides the builder thru each work process and serves as a template for hole locations and diameters. Some jigs include depth gauges so the builder will know the exact depth for an end mill or drill bit. Figure 4.4 depicts an AR-pattern lower receiver blank being cut by a drill press. The degree to which tools are required varies, but, at a minimum, a drill, clamps or vise grip, screwdrivers, a hammer, and punches are needed.

The jigs and fixtures eliminate the need for expensive and complex machine tools and, instead, are designed to work with basic hand and power tools that are available to any consumer at any hardware store. If they chose, builders may use more advanced tools, such as a drill press, instead of a hand drill or router, and this may result in a cleaner or more rapid fabrication; however, it is not absolutely necessary. Figure 4.5 shows an AR-type lower receiver blank installed in a jig. The holes on the top plate are guide holes to aid the builder. The side walls hold everything in place and also provide the holes and dimensions for the trigger and hammer pin and safety/selector holes.

**Figure 4.4** An AR-pattern lower receiver blank in the process of fabrication. The fire-control pocket is being cut out by drilling material away. The jig holds the receiver and guides the cutting. Note the side plates held by the clamps (Image by Boyd Craun; courtesy of AFT).

**Figure 4.5** AR-pattern lower receiver installed in a jig. The blank could be cut using the hand rotary tool, but the end result may not be as clean as using a drill press or router (Image by Boyd Craun; courtesy of AFT).

Fabricating and Assembling                                                                                         69

Figures 4.4 and 4.5 show two different styles of jig used in conjunction with AR-15-type lower receiver blanks of the common type privately made firearms were constructed from. Certain jigs are also compatible with AR-10-style lower receiver blanks, differentiated by a longer magazine well. Figure 4.6 shows a slightly different fixture for an AR-type lower receiver, which is only used to fix the locations and diameters for the safety/selector and auto sear pin holes. This particular fixture is commonly called the "Class II drilling fixture." The safety/selector hole could have a slave pin inserted to hold it in place, in addition to the set screw on the top that mates to the receiver. Other AR-type receiver jigs already have the safety switch hole present but lack the auto sear pin hole. It is a violation of U.S. federal law for an AR-type lower receiver to have a hole drilled to accept an auto sear, even absent the presence of a sear itself. If an AR receiver is encountered that has an auto sear hole present, it should be seized as a contraband item absent evidence that it has been registered or further investigation into the registration status and possession of the firearm can be resolved.

Jigs, tooling, and fixtures are accompanied by printed instructions and matter to guide the builder through the manufacturing processes. Oftentimes, the jigs are demonstrated by the developer using videos hosted through various internet platforms that provide even more detailed instructions. There is an endless amount of instructional, editorial, or commentary postings available online as well. Jigs and fixtures are often supplied as a kit with proper drill bits and end mills, so the builder need not have to source

**Figure 4.6** This fixture shows the locations for the AR-pattern safety/selector hole (low) and the auto sear pin hole (above) (Image from author's collection).

these tools or purchase the wrong type and cause damage to the fixtures, tooling, or the blank. The vendors who sell the jigs and apparatus often sell replacement consumable parts or specify the exact type needed to properly do the job.

A variation of the jig and fixture approach is the tubular-type receiver, which essentially is a length of pipe. So far as receiver blanks are concerned, seamless metal tubing with a template glued to the workpiece is common, providing the builder with instructions showing where to cut and trim. Simple hand tools can be used to create a receiver using a tube-style blank. The author has seen these receiver blanks joined with parts kits to build illicit machine guns; however, this is not inevitable and it is entirely possible to construct a legal firearm on such a completed receiver. Figure 4.7 shows the relative simplicity of the tubular STEN gun style receivers. The receiver was of contemporary manufacture, not wartime vintage, probably constructed from a tube-receiver blank and joined to a STEN parts kit to complete a functional machine gun. The crudeness of the STEN gun, as originally constructed, often makes it difficult to distinguish a wartime original versus a newly made receiver which could be mated to war era components but there is also newly made parts which could be used even as supplies of original components have worn out. There were also numerous wartime copies of the STEN made outside of official British makers. This particular receiver bore a stenciled legend printed laterally down the length of the tubing showing this was modern material. The balance of parts appeared to be original wartime manufacture.

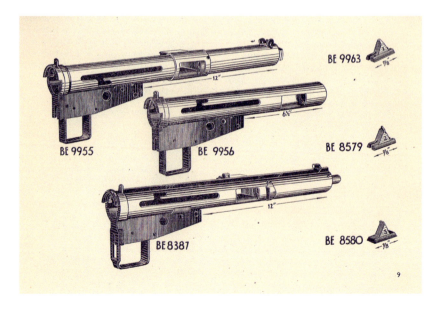

**Figure 4.7** A British wartime schematic showing STEN gun receivers.

Fabricating and Assembling 71

The only other markings were on the magazine well, which showed a wartime maker code and serial number. Like any machine gun which could be either vintage or newly minted origin, it should be thoroughly scrutinized by a competent examiner to determine its construction and likely origin. Figure 4.8 shows a stripped STEN gun receiver. Many other types of firearms could be constructed using tubular receivers, such as the Sterling, which were quite common for mid-century submachine guns. In more recent times, tubular-style receivers have re-emerged in other types of firearms because they are relatively inexpensive to produce.

Side-plate receiver blanks are used to construct semi-automatic versions of Browning-, Maxim-, or Vickers-type machine guns. These types used a box-style receiver that contained the fire-control parts, and the right-side plate of the receiver box was instrumental in the function of said machine gun. The ATF has published results in which it has reviewed semi-automatic versions of the Maxim that use a receiver right-side plate with an approved block, which prevented the installation of full-automatic specification parts.[3] Figure 4.9 is a drawing showing the layout of such a side plate onto a box receiver.

Receiver flats kits are another option for the home builder looking to use a receiver blank. There are kits that offer AK-pattern, MAC type, UZI, and certain CETME/Heckler and Koch receivers that are formed using flats that are folded into shape and use a combination of riveting and/or welding to form the receiver. For sake of illustration, a basic arc welder is very inexpensive and easy to obtain, not to mention the prevalence of welding taught in vocational settings or even more informally at home or on the job. The presence of a welding apparatus even in the home-garage setting would itself be benign. The welding does not have to be perfect, just good enough to hold without having concern for aesthetics. One significant drawback of building from a receiver flat is the tooling and machinery required to bend the flat into shape. As such, home builders would have gravitated toward receivers

**Figure 4.8** STEN-type receiver with trigger housing welded in place. Compare this exemplar to the three styles of receiver depicted in Figure 4.7. This receiver is consistent with the receiver in the middle, part BE 9956 (Image by ATF).

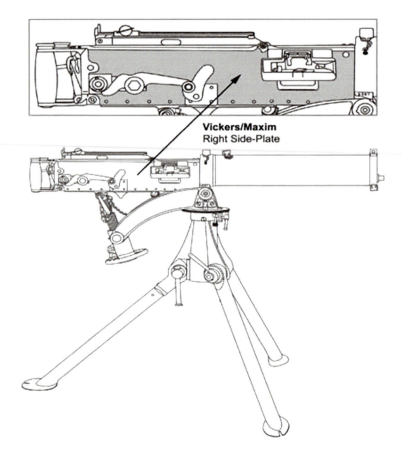

**Figure 4.9** Line drawing of a Vickers-/Maxim-type machine gun. The side plate is considered the receiver on these types of firearms (Image by ATF).

which were partially completed, the so-called "80% receivers"; however, in light of potential reclassifications of such items, the practice of using incomplete blanks, especially when coupled to aids for making the receiver, is likely to diminish greatly.

Regardless of the condition of the receiver blank, there is a variation in the materials and processes and methods that must be applied to fully fabricate the functional receiver. Even within one specific style of receiver, there are variations from supplier to supplier.

## CNC Machinery

The third listed method for manufacturing a receiver is using a CNC machine. A computer numerically controlled machine is a manufacturing

Fabricating and Assembling 73

machine tool, which is operated by a computer. Prior to the marriage of computers with manufacturing machinery, such equipment was operated by skilled workers, machinists. A CNC machine actually encompasses several different styles of machine tools that are used for different purposes, including lathes and mills, among others. Compare the Figures 1.2 and 1.7 to 4.1, 4.10, and 4.11. Contrast the scale of machinery and the overall conditions involved in manufacturing articles in the 1940s versus the 3D printers and desktop CNC[4] machinery of today. The blending of the precision of the electronic computer control and tools began in the 1950s. Currently, a local or networked computer, terminal, and even laptops, smartphones, and tablets that have the installed app or software to interface with the machine tool may command it. The only human interaction required is to install a blank in the machine, power up the machine, and start the program. Inasmuch as the program is properly written, the machine independently executes the commands in sequence and performs a series of cutting operations until the program ends, at which point, presumably, the final product is achieved. At this point, the machine stops. CNC machines themselves have gotten smaller in size, and the software suites do not require prior training or experience with operating machine tools. Computer or robotic control of machinery has expanded to include routers as well. The Ghost Gunner, shown in Figure 4.10, is a CNC machine produced and sold by Defense Distributed, which comes pre-programmed with a catalog of firearm patterns.

In February 2015, common carriers UPS and FedEx each announced they would not accept the Ghost Gunner machine for delivery in their respective networks (Molitch-Hou, 2015). It is not clear whether either carrier would accept any generic CNC machine or 3D printer for shipping or

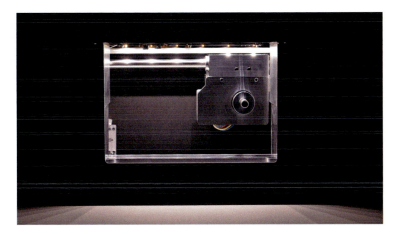

**Figure 4.10** The Defense Distributed Ghost Gunner (Image courtesy of Defense Distributed).

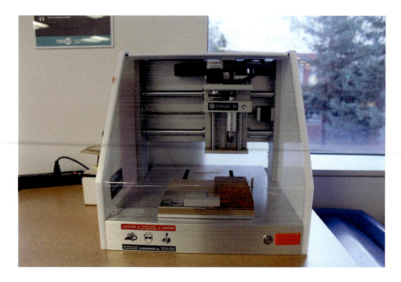

**Figure 4.11** The Carbide 3D CNC machine. The device is capable of cutting polymers, wood, or metals and performing a wide variety of operations (Image courtesy of San Jose Public Library).

their restriction is singular in focus to the Ghost Gunner. Figure 4.11 depicts a desktop CNC machine manufactured by Carbide 3D. This type of machine could easily produce metallic or non-metallic firearm receivers or components, is easily portable, and the manufacturer states it will operate in a Windows or iOS environment. It serves the same function and the Ghost Gunner save the preloaded library of patterns.

## Variations in Receiver Materials

### Machine Steel Receivers

The most traditional material used to construct modern firearms, frames and receivers in particular, is a high-quality machine-grade steel. Various steels have been used, including stainless steel and so-called ordinance steel. The use of high-grade steel alloys ensures a long-lasting and durable product; however, it is expensive to procure and fashion. A recurrent point in this text is the industrial tooling and machinery required to work with such materials, which inevitably led to seeking alternatives.

### Polymer

Nearly every handgun manufacturer currently offers a polymer-framed firearm. This was not always the case. Polymer-framed handguns started appearing in the early 1980s but were met with a great deal of skepticism and even ridicule. Renowned German arms maker Heckler and Koch cataloged a polymer-framed pistol, the VP-70, but it was not a commercial success before production was discontinued. The Glock 17 appeared on the heels of the VP-70, and the Glock line solidified the place of the polymer-frame and spawned countless copies. So far as home gunmakers are concerned, polymer-frame blanks are easy to cut, and there is plenty of aftermarket following to ensure options to finish the build.

## Metal Injection Molding

Metal injection molding is a process that forms parts using granular metal. The process is similar to polymer injection molding: the metal is pressed into a mold of the shape of the object and formed. Frangible ammunition projectiles are made in the same manner, using compressive force to form the projectile or by sintering. In either scenario, a binding material is added to the base material to ensure continuity and strength. Like other materials, alternatives to traditional steel or polymer, components made by metal injection molding are common and, in fact, may be used to produce firearm frames/receivers or blanks.

## Cast or Forged Receivers

A firearm frame or receivers made of castings or forgings are a common alternative to traditional machine steel blanks. The primary reasons for using such castings or forgings are cost and manufacturing expediency. Frames or receivers made by forging appeared as early as the Second World War because they were inexpensive compared to machined parts, could be produced more quickly, and a significantly lower quality material could be used, to the degree that it was suitable for use in a firearm. Zamak, a zinc/aluminum alloy, is a common modern material. The standard AR-pattern firearms may use a forged aluminum receiver, although there are variations on the market including polymer, billet steel, and carbon fiber. At least two types of aluminum alloys are used: 6061 and 7075. Military specifications call for the 7075 alloy to be used, the 6061 is an inferior material but of a lower cost, making it attractive.

## Assembling and Finishing the Self-Made Receiver

Completing a receiver still requires the builder to assemble the firearm. Assembly requires the bringing together the balance of bits and pieces, such as the fire-control parts, barrel, slide, bolts, and anything else specific to the model being constructed, and joined to the functional frame/receiver to complete a fully operable firearm. There is a plethora of commercial outlets for these parts for certain model firearms such as the AR platform, Model 1911 and variants, and Glock-inspired analogs. The successful assembly is predicated on the final receiver being reasonably close to required specifications. If the builder removes too much or too little material in the wrong place; drills holes of the wrong diameter or that are in the wrong place, off-center or misaligned; or there was a programming error on the printer or CNC machine, the receiver may not be reworkable and deemed unsalvageable. A builder may find possible workarounds for such construction errors, but there will be instances in which the project is a total loss. On the other hand, the difference between a result that is aesthetically undesirable or unsightly should not be confused with a receiver that is not functional. A frame/receiver that is slightly out of specification may still function but may present reliability or safety issues.

Another approach to assembling a homemade firearm involves the use of what are generically called "parts kits." Parts kits are compromised of the balance of the components required to assemble a wholly made firearm minus the receiver and barrel.[5] Frequently, parts kits are the residuals of demilled or destroy firearms, meaning the frame, receiver, and barrel of the firearm have been destroyed or rendered unusable to such a degree that they cannot be reconstituted as a firearm or repurposed into another firearm. Frequent approaches used to demill or render these components useless include torch cutting or sawing in such a way as to remove significant gaps of material, making it impossible to reconstruct the receiver while, at the same time, converting the usability of the attached non-gun (non-regulated) parts, i.e., the barrel, stock, sights, and so forth. Parts kits, sourced from foreign or domestic sources, are not uncommon. Figure 4.12 depicts two incomplete parts kits originating from demilled AK-pattern rifles. The once attached receivers were cut in such a way to preserve the barrel, gas system, and barrel trunnion – the rectangular shaped portion at the chamber end of the barrel to which the barrel is riveted – which allows the barrel to be reused. In the AK-pattern firearms, the trunnion is riveted to the receiver. The stock shows the remnants of the trigger guard and shows where the receiver had been torch cut. Nonetheless, the stock was preserved and, like the barrels, could be recycled to attach to another receiver and reused. These kits obviously were imported before the 2005 restrictions were imposed because the barrels are intact.

The ban on parts proved a significant impediment to this approach, as it effectively ended access to certain components that were only obtainable from overseas sources. This was especially true with AK-pattern firearms but could also affect any other firearm that was not made in the United States.

# Fabricating and Assembling

**Figure 4.12** Two AK47 pattern "front ends" and under-folding type metal stock. These parts originated from donor rifles which were "demilled" by destroying the receivers but preserving the salvageable, non-regulated parts. Image from author's collection.

The building of a firearm that used imported parts was already complicated by the 922r[6] requirement, but, in recent years, there has been commitment invested by U.S.-based manufacturers to produce components that would fit offshore firearm patterns. This has negated some of the drawbacks associated with making or remaking foreign-style firearms, principally because of restrictions imposed on importing the parts kits. U.S.-made grips, stocks, triggers, magazines, and other listed articles are readily available and competitively priced.

## Notes

1. The article's author used a Ghost Gunner.
2. There are many different processes behind 3D printing. In the interest of brevity, the generic term 3D printing will be used.
3. See ATF Rul. 2010-3, which clarifies which part of a Vickers-/Maxim-type machine gun is considered the frame or receiver. ATF opined that such a side plate did not constitute a machine gun. These side plates can be used to complete the assembly of this type of firearm with a box-style receiver. In a separate ruling, the ATF opined that the Browning M1919-type firearm is a "portable" firearm. See ATF Ruling 97-2 and identified the M1919A4 and M1919A6 specifically.
4. CNC is a Computerized Numerically Controlled machine, a machine tool operated by a computer program not a human machinist operator.

5. Vintage parts kits exist, which pre-dated the requirement to destroy the barrel. Parts kits may have originated from sources prior to any embargoes that have come to be in place. A comprehensive ban, effective October 10, 2005, had been put into effect by the ATF. However, a notice on the ATF website denoting an update on January 23, 2020, stated parts kits would be permissible to import, excluding machine gun receivers and barrels.
6. 18 U.S.C. § 922(R) "It shall be unlawful for any person to assemble from imported parts any semiautomatic rifle or any shotgun which is identical to any rifle or shotgun prohibited from importation under section 925(d)(3) of this chapter as not being particularly suitable for or readily adaptable to sporting purposes except that this subsection…"

Essentially meaning using more than 10 imported parts from a list of more than 20 parts.

## References

ATF. (2016, September 23). Is a Firearm Illegal If It is Made of Plastic? Retrieved September 22, 2019, from *ATF official website*: https://www.atf.gov/firearms/qa/firearm-illegal-if-it-made-plastic

ATF. (2020, April 6). Are "80%" or "Unfinished" Receivers Illegal? Retrieved from *ATF official website*: https://www.atf.gov/firearms/qa/are-"80"-or-"unfinished"-receivers-illegal

GE. (n.d.). What is Additive Manufacturing? Retrieved July 16, 2020, from *GE*: https://www.ge.com/additive/additive-manufacturing

Molitch-Hou, M. (2015, February 25). FEDEX, UPS REFUSE to Ship Ghost Gunner Gun Milling Machine. Retrieved July 27, 2020, from *3D Printing Industry*: https://3dprintingindustry.com/news/fedex-ups-refuse-to-ship-ghost-gunner-milling-machine-43224/: https://3dprintingindustry.com/news/fedex-ups-refuse-to-ship-ghost-gunner-milling-machine-43224/

# Common Types of Ghost Guns    5

## The Armalite Pattern

The AR-type firearm encompasses a plurality of configurations– from handguns to match quality rifle suitable for long range precision shooting, and in any imaginable caliber. Broadly, the AR lower receiver can be classified into three broad architectures: the AR-10, AR-15, and the AR-9. The AR-10 receiver, relative the other two styles, has a longer magazine well to accommodate the longer ammunition cartridge. The AR-9[1] can be either an offshoot of the AR-15 style, using a magazine block-type to retrofit the smaller dimensioned pistol caliber magazine (such as 9mm, 10mm, etc.), or be a receiver with a magazine well that is physically the same size as the AR-15, but the internal dimensions are cut to suit the smaller size pistol caliber cartridge magazine. Recall image 1.5,which is an AR-15 type lower receiver, note the magazine well is the flat sided portion in front of the trigger. Some internal components will interchange between the three, but some will be caliber-specific.[2] The AR platform was designed from the outset with modularity in mind and has become one of the most versatile and popular firearms ever devised. Ironically, the AR was not always popular and was looked upon with some disdain, having a reputation of unreliability in the Vietnam War, coupled to the symbolic nature of the rifle in the unpopular conflict as the main battle rifle for U.S. forces. It was not a big seller until after the turn of the twenty-first century, by then the basic design was nearly 50 years old. The design passed from Armalite to Colt in the late 1950s, and the original patents for the gun expired in mid-1970s. There are now literally hundreds of companies that produce their own iteration of the basic AR receiver and many dozens of other companies that produce various aftermarket components and accessories. In Chapter 2, the author described the AR-type firearm using separate upper and lower receiver assemblies to form the complete firearm. Figure 5.1 offers a comparison between a raw forging and a finished AR-15-type upper receiver. Such raw forgings, as illustrated, are the blanks which are milled into receivers. There are a finite number of suppliers who produce these, and, hence, they are used by professional gunmakers or by home builders.

The AR-pattern receivers were traditionally formed from a 7075-aluminum forging. There are alternatives, including a 6065 forging. Of the two, 7075 is preferable. Receiver blanks may be sold to the end user with a finish already applied;

**Figure 5.1** AR-15-type upper receiver contrasting the raw aluminum forging to the partially assembled upper. Note the presence of the dust cover door and threads that will mate the barrel to the receiver. The raw forging is in the white, no finish applied. The lower, completed receiver, has been finished in standard black anodizing, but any color can be used (Image from author's collection).

but are also sold "in the white", that is to say with no finishing or coatings applied, leaving the workpiece with its natural appearance. Anodizing is likely the most common finish option for aluminum. The original Armalite platform specified the use of aluminum forgings, alternative materials have included carbon fiber, polymer, and billet steel. Other variations of the basic shape are imagined and bolster the industrial art perspective and some are quite ornate. Figure 5.2 is a graphic depicting a proposed AR-type lower receiver constructed of four pieces bolted together to form the whole receiver, the parts of which were made on a CNC machine. Note the brass fitting at the rear threads to attach the lower receiver extension. The basic appearance and function of the upper and lower receivers is unchanged save for some cosmetic and functional evolutions.

The AR platform functions on direct gas operation (also called "direct impingement"), gas piston, or by blowback. No caliber is appropiate for all three methods, so there is caliber dependency underlying the chosen method. Pistol calibers such as the 9×19mm or 10mm, for example, are blowback, as neither generates sufficient gas pressure to cycle the gas system, instead relying solely on recoil. The direct impingement redirects gas pressure through a gas tube from a gas port in the barrel back into the receiver to push the bolt carrier to the rear. The piston system also bleeds gas pressure from the barrel, but this pressure operates a piston that pushes an operating rod that moves

# Common Types of Ghost Guns

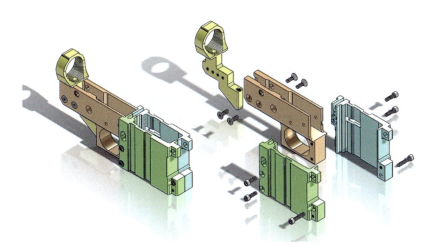

**Figure 5.2** Four-piece AR-15 lower receiver. It is made from three aluminum extrusions (Image by Mitch Barrie under CC BY-ND 2.0).

the bolt carrier. Both the gas impingement and piston methods use a recoil spring and recoil buffer to counteract the rear movement of the bolt carrier group and return the bolt forward to complete the sequence of operation.

The AR receiver blank is probably one of the earliest types defined as a non-gun for home builders. To fabricate a receiver from a non-receiver blank, the fire-control pocket is solid and requires the builder to cut this material away. In addition, the builder must drill three holes through the workpiece sidewalls – the selector/safety switch and holes for the hammer and trigger pins. Now the builder may install the trigger, hammer, and disconnector into the fire-control pocket and install the safety. The balance of subassemblies is installed in sequence, including a magazine catch and bolt catch. The grip is attached with a screw, and the recoil buffer assembly is threaded into place. The fabrication can be done by a CNC machine, drill press, router, or by hand tools. Figure 5.3 shows the raw forging in contrast to the fully machined and finished functional lower receiver. The completed lower is now ready to have the fire control and other parts installed to finish the build.

The AR-type firearm is not a difficult firearm to assemble. The small parts are generally installed using one of different style pins, which are application specific; as well discerning which springs and detents are used in which sub assembly. They are not safely interchangeable and may be the root cause of reliability or safe function issues. The real complications with the AR platform are installing the barrel on the upper receiver and ensuring the gas system is properly tuned. AR-pattern handguns and short-barreled rifles can be particularly troublesome to get the gas system tuned for consistent and reliable operation.

**Figure 5.3** An AR-15-type lower receiver raw forging compared to a completed, finished lower receiver (Image from author's collection).

Another possible reliability issue stems from using the wrong part. Regardless, a functional receiver is exactly that and, as discussed in Chapter 1, a legal determination of functionality is not affected by an improperly assembled build. Generally the small parts follow the original "military specification" so there will be some variation in parts quality but the gun should not require significant gunsmithing to assemble. There is some dissimilarities between the AR-10 and LAR-308 pattern firearm, so not all parts will interchange in this case, and there are certain individual manufacturer variations which are too numerous to individually distinguish here but the reader should be aware variations do exist.

The AR-pattern upper receiver (shown in Figure 5.1) has been treated as a non-regulated component and is obtained either as a wholly assembled unit or in parts from online or face-to-face sales. The builder need only obtain a pre-assembled upper and mate it to the completed lower receiver. The upper and lower receivers are connected by two clevis style pins, called the takedown pin and pivot pin. The pivot pin is located at the front of the lower receiver; the takedown pin is located closer to the rear. The upper receiver assembly contained the bolt carrier group, gas system, and is the attachment for the barrel. Obviously, the barrel must conform to the caliber of the AR that is constructed. The caliber will also have an effect on the bolt carrier group and may require a different extractor to be installed. Many builders prefer to install a barrel themselves, and frequently this is another a weak point which could result in an unsafe gun to fire. Many instructional videos, blog or forum postings, or other published "guidance" do not specify a

# Common Types of Ghost Guns

torque value for the barrel and, instead, fasten the barrel to the receiver using a thread lock adhesive in lieu of properly torqueing the barrel using a torque wrench with a gauge. Others may forgo either entirely or rely on hand tightening. Obviously, if the barrel separates from the upper receiver when firing this creates a significant safety hazard.

The legalities of an AR-type build are generally focused on two points: a legally configured firearm, i.e. a short barreled rifle, and the making of an unregistered machine gun. Recall the firearm types identified in Chapter 3. Builders must assemble a legally configured pistol, rifle, or shotgun from the receiver unless the receiver has been properly registered, such as in the case of a short-barreled rifle. AR-type receivers are often used as the basis of a large-format handgun, as shown in Figure 1.5, in which case, a pistol stabilizing brace or similar apparatus is used in lieu of a stock. Prior to the pistol brace, AR tubular receiver extensions were often coated in neoprene for comfort. Standard fixed or collapsible style stocks were not easily fitted onto this type of extension. Recently proposed regulatory changes by ATF, if enacted, are going to change parameters for pistol stabilizing braces and they are likely to disappear from the marketplace.

There are at least four methods known to convert a semi-automatic AR into a reliably functioning machine gun. Contrast Figures 5.4 and 5.5 and notice the

**Figure 5.4** A semi-automatic AR-15-type lower receiver with the trigger, hammer, and disconnector installed. To the rear of the hammer is an elevated "shelf" that would prevent the installation of a standard full auto sear. In addition, there is no sear pin hold to set the sear into place. A drop in auto sear, such as one shown in Figure 3.4, does not require a pin or other modifications to install which would betray its presence. (Image from author's collection).

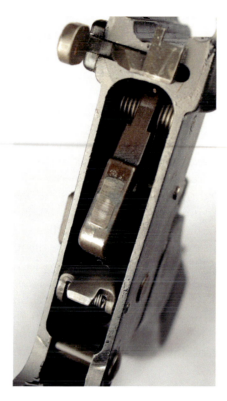

**Figure 5.5** A fully automatic AR-15-type lower receiver. Situated behind the hammer is the full auto sear, which is not present in the receiver shown in Figure 5.4. The auto sear is installed using an independent pin (Image from author's collection).

differences in the installed parts. In Figure 5.5, a military specification full auto sear is used. Alternatively, drop in auto sears (see Figure 3.4), Lightning Links, or other like devices have been used to "trick" the AR's internal mechanisms into firing in full auto mode. Drop in auto sears and Lightning Links are considered to be machine guns, even though they are small parts, and can be installed in any host; however, these parts must be serial numbered and registered.

One of the draws of the AR platform is its adaptability as a whole but also for its constituent components. At this point, all the parts which compromise an AR firearm, with the exception of the lower receiver, are unregulated and therefore are reasonably inexpensive and easily obtainable. Figure 4.3 shows an AR-style trigger which was created by additive manufacturing. Even if such small parts became regulated or in venues where such small gun parts are already restricted from purchase and possession, they can easily be made on a 3D printer. Compare the triggers in Figure 4.3 to the trigger in Figure 3.8, made by a professional manufacturer by traditional methods. Figures 5.4 and 5.5 show the trigger installed.

Common Types of Ghost Guns 85

# The Model 1911 and Variants

The Model 1911 was created by John Moses Browning, who designed more firearms in his lifetime than any other single person. The 1911 was the definitive iteration of a series of designs that Browning had started devising at the turn of the nineteenth into the twentieth century. The design is most closely associated with Colt, often simply known as the "Colt .45"; however, the 1911 and its iterations has been in continuous production for more than 100 years, and many brand names have made their own version of the basic design. The 1911 has an enduring reputation as a tinkerer's gun, one that must be assembled and fitted by hand, which was how guns were made when it was designed more than 100 years ago. Figures 5.6 and 5.7 show a commercially made 1911A1 handgun. Factory made 1911s use steel for the slide and frame; however, aluminum is used in home builder receiver blanks, as it is easier to cut and is strong enough to form the basis of a reliable firearm.

The 1911 has had subtle changes made to the design over the years, and many companies have taken their own artistic liberties to the basic design. At this point in history, there is no real standard 1911 per se; however, should an individual decide to craft their own 1911, they will find a wide range of parts from a wide variety of sources. Due to sutbtle variations in tolerances and the degree of exactness each part will fit with others, practically all internal parts will likely require some degree of "gunsmith fitting". The 1911 is a popular

**Figure 5.6** The left side of a 1911A1 pistol. This side shows the slide lock, safety lever, and magazine release button. This 1911A1 is of modern manufacture but is styled in tribute to World War II-era pistols made for government contract (Image courtesy of Auto Ordnance).

**Figure 5.7** The right side of a 1911A1 pistol (Image courtesy of Auto Ordnance).

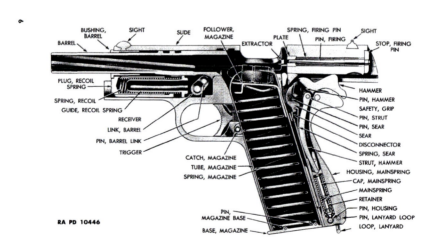

**Figure 5.8** A schematic showing the M1911a1 small parts. Image from U.S. War Department TM 9 1295.

choice for home builders because it is such a tolerance-centric design. The 1911 home builder can be confounded by the differences in specifications and tolerances between frame cutting instructions and parts supplied by different manufacturers. For example, there are three different specifications for the firing pin tips, which are dependent upon the caliber of the pistol, and 1911 pistols have been made in a wide range of calibers, .45 ACP being the most common. Figure 5.8 is taken from the pages of a War Department

# Common Types of Ghost Guns

Ordnance Manual on the M1911 and M1911A1 pistols. The schematic shows the arrangement and nomenclature of the small parts contained in the frame and slide. Figure 5.9 shows the slide, barrel, barrel bushing, recoil spring, and slide lock.

The 1911 pattern frame blank is made into a receiver by cutting critical areas. The elevated top rear portion of the frame blank is cut to create the frame rails or where the slide attaches to the frame. Within the frame is an area called the *barrel seat* – located inside the frame roughly above the trigger guard and forward of the magazine well – is also cut. Two holes are drilled into the side walls above the gip backstrap for the hammer and sear pins. Many automatic pistol receiver kits follow this approach with some variations to account for differences in the design.

Once the cutting is completed, the builder installs the small parts with minute adjustments as needed. The slide is a non-regulated component and is married to the frame. Figure 5.10 shows a very precise engagement between the slide and frame.

## Glock Pattern Handguns

The Glock handgun, at times controversial, has certainly made its mark in the history of gun development. Even before the proliferation of self manufacture

**Figure 5.9** A 1911A1 slide taken down showing the barrel, slide details, recoil spring, and slide stop. Inside the slide and not shown are the extractor, firing pin, and firing pin stop (Image from author's collection).

**Figure 5.10** A view from the back of a 1911 pistol showing the precision fit between the slide and frame. Aficionados of the 1911 look for a close fit between parts as a measure of quality (Image courtesy of Kimber America).

receiver blank kits, the Glock had a large aftermarket following, custom slides, barrels, and triggers, in particular, all touting some performance advantage over the original Glock design. It should, therefore, come as no surprise that the Glock-type receiver has emerged as the basis for a home build. Broadly, a Glock-type receiver is fashioned by drilling pin holes for the trigger housing pin, locking block pin, trigger pin and cutting the rails for the slide. Some minor surface treatments and dressing may be in order for a proper fit. After completing the receiver, Glock factory or aftermarket parts are installed, and the pistol slide is joined to the frame. Glock factory or compatible aftermarket magazines may be used. Figure 5.11 shows a Glock constructed using a self-made "ghost gun" receiver that has been coupled to what appears to be an original equipment Glock slide to complete the build. The image was taken during a press conference, and there are other examples of homemade firearms as well. The red plastic rectangle appears to be a Glock-frame-type jig. Of note are an AR-type firearm and other firearms-related matter on the table. It would appear substantial numbers of new Glock handguns are purchased strictly for the original equipment slide and barrel; large numbers of frames are found for sale thru second hand sources. It appears in Figure 5.11 the gun uses a Glock factory slide mated to a privately made receiver.

# Common Types of Ghost Guns

**Figure 5.11** Firearms are pictured during a press conference inside the Governor's Reception Room at the Pennsylvania state capitol building on Monday, December 16, 2019, outlining a new legal opinion from the Attorney General's Office addressing the classification of "80% receivers," which are most commonly used to make unserialized ghost guns. The opinion clarifies that, under the Pennsylvania Uniform Firearms Act, these receivers are properly classified as firearms in Pennsylvania. This opinion, in accordance with the Commonwealth Attorneys Act, was issued to tackle the growing use of untraceable ghost guns and to further assist law enforcement officials to protect people and save lives (Image Flickr. Creative Commons).

## Ruger 10/22

The Ruger 10/22 has been a staple "plinker" gun that multiple generations of shooters learned to shoot with. It is a design that is reliable, inexpensive, and has proven to be very versatile. The 10/22 has long enjoyed an aftermarket following, so it stands to reason that it would become a popular option for home building as well. The basic 10/22-type receiver blank requires the builder to drill appropriate diameter holes in the proper locations. The finalized receiver can then be mated with any original equipment manufacturer (OEM) or aftermarket barrels and stocks for the 10/22 in addition to the receiver parts – bolt and fire-control parts. There is a large aftermarket following for the design, so parts of all styles are readily accessible. Like the AR-type, a 10/22 pattern rifle or pistol can be constructed.

## The AK-Type Firearm

The original AK-47 was designed during the Second World War by Mikael Kalashnikov and adopted for Soviet military service in 1947. The original AK receiver was made of machined steel, but this was short-lived, and the design was transitioned to a stamped receiver and officially designated the AKM-47, "M" for "modernized." In general speech, the AKM terminology is not used, and any firearm in the lineage or resemblance of the AK-47 is simply called the AK. The basic function of the rifle remained the same, but the stamped receiver version was considerably lighter to carry and certainly less expensive and faster to manufacture. As the AK was taken into service by many different nations many of whom chose to manufacture their own variant, which inevitably led to certain localized adaptations such that not all AK parts and receivers interchange with all others. The magazine and ammunition remained common. The AK's simplicity in operation is often mistaken for its complications in manufacturing. The AK has critical tolerances in certain locations, and an inexperienced builder may end up with a less than desirable finished project that could require minor, moderate, or substantial reworking to bring the build to success, and even still it may never be right. The design is especially finicky around the headspace. The experience of the home builder and the AK has been mixed. AK receiver kits have been of mix quality. Parts kits originate from various nations and, due to irregularity in manufacturing, some receiver kits do not mesh with the parts kit. The AK builder had to contend with the 922(r)-parts compliance issue, which has been remedied by U.S. companies manufacturing AK parts. There are several styles of AK receiver blanks available. The first style is called a "flat" and is literally flat, requiring the builder to bend the receiver walls into shape. The flat-style blank has many of the rivet holes already present as an offset for the builder having to bend the receiver into shape. AK receivers are made in at two different wall thickness, 1mm and 1.6mm. The 1.6mm is most preferable of the two. Poor metalugry also plagues the AK receiver, with softer metals subject to warpage even from the heat generated during routine use. The flat-style blank is harder to work with because it requires the builder anneal (apply heat) and then form the flat around a jig to the proper shape. It is very easy to overheat the flat and imperfectly shape it; therefore, it is likely many builders will simply opt for an 80% AK receiver blank, which is already pre-shaped and go with drilling holes. Most of the AK parts are riveted in place, including the fire-control parts, trigger guard, and the barrel trunnion with the barrel already installed. In lieu of riveting, this process is simplified by using screws to attach the trigger guard, cross member, and barrel trunnion into place. It is very likely that considerable hand fitting and adjustment to the receiver rails will be required. Again, the diversity of specifications of

# Common Types of Ghost Guns

parts and access to parts challenges the AK build. Like the AR platform, the AK can be configured as a handgun or rifle.

## The Liberator

The Liberator is at the root of the modern ghost gun movement. The name Liberator is derived from a historical firearm of the same name. The original Liberator was a crude, simple single-shot, striker fired pistol that was widely distributed to various resistance movements in Axis occupied countries during World War II. The original Liberator was made of sheet metal by the Guide Lamp Corporation, formally a Division of General Motors. The modern Liberator pistol design was conceived by Cody Wilson as a 3D-printed gun that used a common nail as a firing pin. The design was not likely to win any beauty contests with its crude, clunky appearance, but it did prove the concept of a functional firearm which could be made by additive manufacturing with minimal, basic other materials used to complete it, i.e. the nail. Figure 5.12 depicts the Liberator in a computer modeling image. Figure 5.13 depicts the printed components of the Liberator. The Victoria & Albert Museum in London, England holds three Liberators in its collection, one of which is fractured apparently from firing; which puts to rest the questions of

**Figure 5.12** Computer generated model of the Liberator pistol (Image by Greg. Creative Commons).

**Figure 5.13** 3D printed Liberator parts (Image by Mirko Tobias Schäfer. Creative Commons).

whether anyone actually made a Liberator or Liberator inspired printed firearm, and if one had ever actually been fired. Images purporting to be virtual models of variants of the basic Liberator concept are seen online.

## Tubular Receiver Firearms

During the course of gun-making history, many different designers devised similar firearms. For a period of time tubular receiver were common, especially for submachine guns. To clarify, the submachine gun is a firearm capable of fully automatic fire and fires a pistol caliber cartridge, such as 9x19mm, .45 ACP, 7.62x25mm Tokarov, and so forth. The British STEN gun, Russian PPS, German MP-40, and Swedish Suomi are three examples of submachine guns that use tubular receivers. The tube has cuts made to accommodate parts attached to it that are easily spot welded into place. The balance of parts could be surplused from existing stockpiles, destroyed firearms which were parted out, or newly made (refer to Figures 4.7 and 4.8 for examples of tube receivers).

## Suppressors

Suppressors are one of several types of firearms regulated in the United States under the National Firearms Act. Although not a firearm as defined as others are – a device capable of expelling a projectile under force of explosive – a suppressor and even suppressor components absent a complete suppressor are defined as a firearm, therefore it has not been possible for even owners of legitimately registered and possessed suppressors to hold spare parts for repair or replacement of worn components. An exception to this are end caps which mate to the barrel of the host firearm, to mate to different threading. A suppressor can be fabricated by an unlicensed entity; however, unlike other privately made firearms, it must be registered and its construction approved before undertaking manufacture. Suppressors, often called *silencers* are basically a canister, frequently cylindrically shaped although other shapes do exist, containing a series of baffles, called a stack, a mono-block internal structure, or some other type of compartmentalized chambering setup that is designed to abate the sound of gunfire. Suppressors vary greatly in their effectiveness; however, they do not necessarily perform to the degree depicted in movies or television. Similar devices that are not used in conjunction with firearms are not legally defined as suppressors, such as a device installed on a non-gun (i.e., a muzzleloader, airsoft gun, or a paintball gun)[3], blank fire adapter, or a non-functional, inert suppressor analog, whether it is solid or has a bore which can be fired thru. SilencerCo had previously manufactured a muzzleloader, called the Maxim 50, that had a sound-reducing device attached. Since a muzzloader is not legally defined a firearm, the attached sound reduction device, so long as remained attached to such a muzzleloader, would not be a firearms suppressor. There are numerous companies that manufacture suppressors as normal course of business and market the items to individual consumers, law enforcement agencies, or military entities; however, there are individuals who prefer to make their own or are interested in research and experimentation into sound moderation theories offered by suppressors. Figure 2.7 depicts a commercially manufactured suppressor. Improvised suppressors have been the topic of many underground publications that offer detailed guidance on the underlying principle and methods for clandestinely constructing expedient devices and attaching such suppressor to a host firearm. Additive manufacturing has proven a viable means of producing durable suppressors, and the method has been embraced by several manufacturers.

Craft or improvised suppressors are often fashioned from pre-existing, mundane non-firearm items. Commonly anything cylindrical in shape and somewhat durable, such as automotive in-line fuel or oil filters, two liter bottles, small engine mufflers, water filters such as those used in refrigerators, and basic seamless metal or alumnium tubing. The author has seen PVC or metal pipe used, a smaller diameter bore set into the pipe body, and the balance of the device filled with all kinds of materials including fiberglass insulation, metal washers, and other like matter found at the local hardware or craft store. Once the housing has been settled upon, the craft builder need only to decide the internal set up and how to mate the improvised device to a host firearm. The so-called *solvent trap* is viewed by many as a gateway item from which a homemade suppressor could be fashioned. Contrary to popular belief, the solvent trap concept has been around for quite a few years. The solvent trap serves the bona fide purpose of acting as an aid in cleaning a firearm. When cleaning the bore (interior portion of the barrel) and internal spaces within the firearm, it is often necessary to pour a liquid cleaning agent through the bore and, without some method of capturing the solvent for reuse or proper disposal, these chemicals would be spilled out. However, a solvent trap could be used as the basis from which to construct a firearm suppressor. Because the trap serves as the housing, the builder merely installs some style of baffling or whatever other internal apparatus they desire to complete the build.

In the author's estimation, there has been more advancement in the field of suppressors in the last 20 years then in the prior ninety. Certainly part of this can be explained by the increased use of suppressors in recent conflicts and the demand for better, more effective suppressors; but this is in no small part contributed to by many individual tinkerers in competitive spirit to outdo one another. Additive manufacturing is likely to further accelerate this as it is even easier and more cost effective to produce suppressors, and, unlike machine guns, will certainly provide the impetus to the next generation of suppressors.

## Original Designs and Hybrid Patterns

So far, the focus has been on established firearm designs. Private firearm builders are simply creating their own copy of an existing design. With the exception of suppressors, and only if there is patent protection in place, the aforementioned designs discussed in this chapter have expired patents, and, therefore, there is no intellectual property infringement. Creating new and novel firearms or seeking to improve existing ideas is in keeping with the spirit of homemade firearms. History shows numerous examples of firearm designs that became historical benchmarks that were created not by government arsenals or privately owned arms manufacturers but by private individuals. John Garand, the inventor of the main battle rifle carried by U.S. Armed Forces in the Second World War, developed his namesake gun, the M1 Garand, mainly on his own. Only late in the stages of the rifle's development was Garand employed by the U.S. government, which allowed him to concentrate on perfecting the design and meeting the Army's requirements. John Browning did have business relations with various gunmakers during his lifetime but developed firearms principally as a private person. Figure 5.14 depicts a prototype firearm that was manufactured by a non-regulated person. It is obvious the design is inspired by the AR-type lower receiver.

# Common Types of Ghost Guns

**Figure 5.14** Prototype Blackstar Arms rifle (Image by Mitch Barrie. Creative Commons).

Nonetheless, it seems plausible, if not likely, that the privately made firearm movement will move toward the hybrid design as the focus of future projects. If proposed changes actually go into effect, it appears from the language within the ATF 2021R-05 proposal one of the main points is to redefine receiver blanks and workpieces, especially in kit form and in full consideration of supporting materials and instructions, guidance, and tooling, as firearms. Hybrid firearm designs offer a possible workaround to the proposed *newspeak* terms by avoiding the use of a receiver blank and accompanying support materials. In fact even as the rulemaking proposal seeks to redefine a functional firearm frame or receiver to include, "'partially complete' for purposes of this definition 'means a forging, casting, printing, extrusion, machined body, or similar article that has reached a stage in manufacture where it is clearly identifiable as an unfinished component part of a weapon.'" (ATF, 2021).

Since additive manufacturing processes produce an item "from the ground up", rather than relying on blanks or workpieces which are milled and cut into shape, it could effectively avoid rule changes as additive manufacturing starts with nothing except basic materials in an ordinary state and create from nothing the project piece. Additive manufacturing could just as easily construct replacement car radio knobs as it could make gun parts, therefore regulating the technology is, practically speaking, an impossibility. This may be of special concern in places where not only guns are strictly regulated, if not completely prohibited, as anyone's commonly available technology could produce completed, functional firearms. Firearms are one thing, access to ammunition, also a potential impediment in places where ammunition sales are carefully restricted, are also potentially rendered null by 3D printed ammunition, which has been on the table since at least 2020.

There are not special, firearm-centric supplementary tools, jigs, or other apparatus required to specify a firearm from a 3D printer. Many hybrid designs rely on certain items which are either generalized pieces of hardware such as nuts, bolts, fasteners, and the like or certain firearm specific parts and accessories which currently remain unregulated, such as a grip or grip panels. One iteration of the Cody Wilson Liberator pistol, previously described in this chapter, used a standard US military style M16 style hand grip. Other iterations of the Liberator appear to use a hand grip fabricated using the same additive manufacturing process and materials as the balance of the Liberator itself, save the nail which acts as the firing pin. A cursory review of certain internet sources revealed innumberable proof of concepts of various guns which fall under this hybrid type category made using additive manufacturing processes.

## Notes

1. AR-9 is used generically here to identify Armalite-pattern lower receivers that use pistol caliber cartridges,
2. There are different variants within the AR-10 platform that do not allow for absolute interchangeability between parts, and some companies use proprietary designs that limit which parts will fit,
3. See ATF Ruling 2005-4: "Certain integral devices intended to diminish the report of paintball guns are not 'firearm silencers' or 'firearm mufflers' under the Gun Control Act of 1968 or the National Firearms Act."

## Reference

ATF. (2021). *Definition of "Frame or Receiver" and Identification of Firearms.*

# Investigative Considerations

# 6

Over the course of this text, several cases involving homemade firearms were used to give sense and depth to the subject. The profiled investigations stemmed from different occurrences – homicide, sting operations, and long-term investigations into criminal activities – that required time to obtain sufficient evidence to bring the case to fruition. Firearm investigations may start through proactive efforts in which authorities actively seek to uncover potential violations. More commonly, firearms cases are reactive, in which, through happenstance, authorities come across possible firearms crime peripheral to a primary offense that is under investigation or has been uncovered. An easy example is the narcotics trade. Inevitably, where there are narcotics, there are firearms – always a bad combination. In the early 1980s, south Florida was a crossroads for cocaine trafficking from South America through Central America and the Caribbean into the United States. Miami, in particular, was awash in cocaine, and soon every imaginable type of firearm from anywhere in the world was showing up as the level of violence between rivals escalated. With hundreds of millions of dollars at play, money was no object to acquire firearms in furtherance of trafficking cocaine. With shipments of cocaine measured by the ton flowing in, what was the big deal to throw in a pile of machine guns with the cocaine being smuggled? Consider the scale of investigations. A single traffic stop may yield contraband and firearms contained within the vehicle after a lawful search is made; a search warrant is executed at a residence after a month-long investigation, whereas complex long-term investigations focused on dismantling a crime syndicate require more time and resources to build a case on the principles and may involve multiple agencies, if a task force has not already been formed. Figure 6.1 shows a contemporary multi-agency operation involving narcotics and firearms. Given the complexities of many investigations and the potential for concurrent or overlapping jurisdiction, multi-agency or task force–type approaches, if properly managed and the correct talent brought in, can be very effective at dismantling criminal enterprises.

Because firearms are legal consumer goods, they are not necessarily contraband; however, there are ample instances in which firearms are pertinent to the case evidence. Therefore, firearms could be treated as *fruits* or *instruments* of crime. This statement, in and of itself, is complicated by the patchwork of various laws, as what is legal in one venue may not be legal in another.

DOI: 10.4324/9781003044499-6

**Figure 6.1** Investigators from multiple federal and local law enforcement agencies, including U.S. Immigration and Customs Enforcement's (ICE) Homeland Security Investigations (HSI), the Drug Enforcement Administration, and the Pima County Sheriff's Department, executed numerous search and arrest warrants in southern Arizona, dismantling a local drug trafficking organization suspected of distributing and selling heroin, marijuana, and various firearms (Image by Charles Reed; courtesy of ICE).

In the aforementioned scenarios, firearms possessed in connection with the narcotics trade could be determined to be violations of law.

## Investigative Methods and Techniques for Interdicting Contraband Arms

### Traffic Stops

Trafficking contraband and transporting persons engaged in criminal enterprise requires the physical movement of the items from Point A to Point B. Without the ability to move it, the contraband is sequestered where it lay, essentially rendered inert and a non-factor; in some ways, perhaps, preventing events from ever developing that were fueled by the presence of drugs and especially with criminal handling of firearms. It is very hard to sell narcotics when it is difficult to transport them and there is always the chance of the movement being intercepted.

Much ado has been made of law enforcement efforts to interdict contraband by intercepting it in transit, in other words, the traffic stop. The protection of privacy for private property (homes, businesses, conveyances) is among those that are most sacrosanct, requiring a search warrant or one of a very few and narrow warrant exceptions to enter into and conduct a search for evidence. However, once contraband leaves the sanctuary of private property and enters the public space, albeit in a private conveyance, it offers a window of opportunity to interdict the contraband. There has been a lot of criticism directed at "pretextual"[1] traffic stops for quite some time, even in spite of the practice being upheld by the U.S. Supreme Court in *Whren v. United States*.[2] In more recent times, the broader theme of realigning the role and scope of police in the United States has prompted certain venues to eliminate the pretextual traffic stop altogether.

> The Oregon Supreme Court ruled last November police could no longer pull someone over for a broken taillight or failure to signal, then ask unrelated questions, such as asking for consent to search the car for illegal drugs or guns.
>
> (Mercer, 2020)

> The Berkeley City Council voted in favor of a proposal to replace police enforcement of traffic violations with unarmed city employees.
>
> (Schneider, 2020)

In spite of some contemporary theories critical of the practice, traffic stops are proven to be an effective means by which law enforcement interdicts the movement of contraband and has the peripheral effect as a crime prevention measure. One need not be a criminologist or law enforcement professional to recognize the truth in this statement; there is empirical evidence aplenty to be had by merely watching any of the number of reality-based police shows to see how seemingly "common" or "routine" traffic stops yield all sorts of contraband and often in substantial quantities. The theory has been offered that, because traffic stops are so effective, this is one of the major motivating factors behind efforts to discredit and abolish the practice, thereby paving the way for unfettered movement of contraband.

## Controlled Buys

Controlled buys are an investigative technique whereupon authorities gain the confidence of a "source" from which to obtain contraband. The deal is negotiated to make the purchase and the particulars of the arrangement are agreed; details such as where to meet, when the meeting will happen, and of course the payment arrangements. and either an undercover law enforcement officer or an agent acting on behalf of law enforcement, usually a confidential informant, procures said contraband. After the sale is made, the procurer remands control of the matter to waiting law enforcement. Customarily, the event occurs under some type of direct surveillance for evidentiary and safety reasons. A controlled buy may result in the immediate arrest of the target who just made the sale, but, often, an arrest is not made, and, instead, the transaction is allowed to proceed thru conclusion as if it were a routine deal to allow the investigation to further mature. Often, many controlled buys are made in increasing quantity as rapport is established, allowing more evidence to be accumulated to further the case. When dealing with firearms and related matter, the evidentiary value of the purchased article must often be confirmed beyond the mere representations made by the seller as to what the item is. Controlled buys involving firearms can be a tricky situation – if law enforcement acts in haste, they could blow the operation if erroneous conclusions are made about what has been purchased. The author is familiar with this exact situation transpiring. If agents intend to make a controlled buy on a suspected contraband firearm, it is strongly encouraged they be thoroughly briefed on the initial indicators and other visual cues to make initial, presumptive determination of how the offered article corresponds to what was offered for sale. Furthermore, if possible, a credentialled subject matter expert should be available as soon as practical after the sale is made. This expert should then perform whatever examinations are needed to ascertain the legality of the exhibit, which allows the investigative team to determine if this is a viable operation or is a red herring.

> The author had the opportunity to brief undercover operatives who had set up a meeting to acquire certain firearms. The undercover operatives sought specific information and guidance about the prospective firearms they were going to be offered. The author was told what firearms were offered and was able to provide specific features and indicators to these undercover agents. Having certain insights and knowledge were going to give the buyers, in this case undercover agents, fluency in the materials and enhance their credibility.

> To the point of a red herring, the author is familiar with an incident in which a confidential informant (CI) offered to make an introduction

between the handler and a party who was selling "machine guns." The CI had been signed up for narcotics work, but the team was obviously interested in the introduction and the prospect of making a buy. The CI set up the introduction and, after a series of meetings, a sale was arranged. As it turns out, the firearm being sold was a semi-automatic rifle. Misrepresentations or false impressions had misled investigators into buying an otherwise legal firearm. Firearm misinformation permeates all levels of society, no one is immune. This illustration merely supports the author's assertion to have a credentialled SME at hand and reminds us that perception and representation are not true depictions of reality. People see a firearm which overtly resembles something they see on the news, in movies, and video games and assume it must be one in the same, which was apparently the case here; someone merely saw what they perceived to be a "machine gun", based upon perceptions perhaps; however, since one can never trust a confidential informant, the true reasoning, by blissful ignorance or deliberate motivation will never be known.

## Controlled Delivery

Controlled deliveries are another method for obtaining evidence. Essentially, parcels containing contraband are intercepted in transit and then delivered to the destination under the surveillance of authorities, who act once the delivery is completed and a recipient has taken custody of the parcel from the carrier. Because the parcels were intercepted, the contents are known and determined to be contraband before being allowed to proceed through the delivery process. The end recipient would have no advanced knowledge of the screening and, therefore, is blissfully unaware a controlled delivery is taking place. In this example, the common carrier includes the postal service or other common carriers who deliver parcels to homes and businesses. A variant of a controlled delivery occurs when the contraband is intercepted while being delivered in a private conveyance. If authorities are able to get the delivery person (sometimes called a 'mule') to cooperate with them, they may allow the delivery to occur under direct surveillance and allow the transaction to be completed. Generally, when the delivery is completed, authorities will move in to secure the evidence and take into custody the person who took possession. The scene is cleared and secured once a search warrant for the premises is obtained in anticipation of finding additional evidence or fruits of criminal activity. At the very least the materials that were delivered will be seized. Given the particulars of a controlled delivery, it is almost certain authorities will have ample probable cause to justify a judge or magistrate issuing the warrant.

## Can a Criminal Manufacture a Firearm?

In short, yes, it is done. One of the central arguments made against the privately made firearm (PMF) is the practice bypasses controls placed on the retail sales of firearms and, therefore, a loss of control over who can obtain the firearm thru ordinary commerce. This argument suggests a prohibited person would simply opt to make or obtain through proxy a firearm under the veil of anonymity because they know they cannot obtain a firearm through an over-the-counter retail dealer. An added dimension to this discussion includes such a person crafting a prohibited firearm. However, illegally obtaining a firearm has never seemed to have proven to be an impediment to a determined criminal, never mind the fact that there is no known method that has proven effective at keeping a firearm away from a prohibited person save their own personal desire to avoid breaking another law. There are multiple avenues that criminals use to obtain firearms in the furtherance of their criminal enterprise, including the black market, straw purchases, first-hand theft, or receipt of stolen firearms taken by others. Furthermore, there is no effective deterrent, other than a good conscience and a desire to be law abiding, to prevent any person from making or possessing a prohibited firearm. In many of the cases illustrated in this text, all part of press releases and matters of public record, persons were already prohibited from possessing firearms, and it is apparent that these persons had no regard for the fact they were breaking the law by possessing firearms while committing other offenses.

## Lost or Stolen Firearms

Lost and stolen firearms have always found eager buyers on the street. This is true anywhere and at any time – no matter which nation, language spoken, or acceptable medium of exchange that is used – cash, narcotics, food, or another barter, all of which are a convenient quid pro quo. Obtaining firearms in this manner is not difficult. The criminal element operating in any society is well networked, and anyone looking for something in particular can generally be pointed in the right direction to the extent that they are considered trustworthy and, especially, if there has already been introductions and a rapport established. Great Britain, for all intents and purposes, has long banned private ownership and possession of firearms. It has been a long-standing practice for British constables to go about their duties unarmed, although this generality is no longer absolutely true, as there are armed constables to respond to situations which arise requiring an armed presence.

On December 26, 2003, David Bieber shot and killed Police Constable Ian Broadhurst and wounded Police Constables Neil Roper and James Banks. The incident occurred in Leeds, England, after Broadhurst and Roper encountered Bieber sitting in an illegally parked stolen car. Bieber, unbeknownst the two constables, was living under the assumed name Nathan Coleman in England and was a fugitive wanted for murder in the United States. Bieber was armed with a 9mm handgun and, later, a search of his property uncovered several hundred rounds of ammunition, all of which is strictly prohibited in England. Nonetheless, a person living illegally in the country under an alias was able to obtain and maintain possession of a firearm and ammunition on an island nation with some of the strictest firearms laws in the world.

In Chapter 1, the role and significance of technology that has undoubtedly helped fuel the interest in self-manufacturing firearms was discussed. Here again, consider the accessibility and proliferation of the internet with respect to firearms. The dark web has become the next black-market bazaar for all types of contraband and questionable materials, firearms among them. Whether moving firearms across town or trafficking across international borders, the internet offers a means of communication and networking with a high degree of, but not absolute, anonymity. The more porous the border, the easier it is to move firearms from nation to nation. Coupled with numerous methods of moving cash payments quickly and seamlessly, such as cryptocurrencies or cash transfer apps, all types of firearms are, at least theoretically, obtainable. The extent of actual deals which result in the sale of arms over such platforms is highly speculative. These platforms are merely an extension of the real world, there are scam artists looking to rip people off, offering guns for sale but never actually having any of the promised merchandise, let alone any intention of delivering once payment is received. Skepticism and suspicion confound sales; buyers and sellers do not know who they are actually dealing with and may believe they are being lured into a sting operation by law enforcement. Pre-arranged meetings to transfer the goods may result in one party robbing the other party, having never had the intention of seeing the deal thru, it was merely a convenient way of robbing a person who likely will not report the incident to the police since they would be incriminating themselves as an active participant in a crime.

## Straw Sales

The *straw sale* is another approach that is used by a prohibited person to obtain a firearm. A 2016 article published by the National Rifle Association Blog stated, "ATF has said that nearly half of illegally trafficked firearms originate with straw purchasers, all of whom pass background checks" (McHale, 2016). A straw sale involves the use of an accomplice, a person who is not prohibited from making a retail firearm purchase. The accomplice who will make the purchase could be a romantic partner, relative, friend, or other "useful idiot" in a quid pro quo for drugs, money, or other considerations as compensation for their role. The straw buyer may just as easily be a willing accomplice. The straw buyer may or may not be accompanied by the actual recipient into the sales situation. In fact, many straw buyers make the buy unaccompanied to avoid arousing suspicion or calling attention to the prohibited party. The straw buyer is coached on what to purchase and provided the funds to complete the sale. Smart phones only make it easier, as images and text messaging can be instantly shared under the guise of "friendly advice from a friend" or "I am showing someone what I am doing." The straw buyer purchases the firearm under the pretense that they are purchasing it for themselves, certifying the same under the penalty of perjury on the necessary paperwork, and submit to the background check. Assuming everything goes according to plan, the straw buyer takes possession of the firearm, after any mandatory waiting periods, and hands the firearm off to the other party. There are certain clues and *indicators* retailers use to detect potential straw sales that prompt them to clarify the potential sale before proceeding or simply decline the sale. Common indicators include:

- Excessive coaching or focusing attention of the "buyer" by the "helpful companion" toward a particular item.
- One party is completing the paperwork, but the other party produces the method of payment.
- The "buyer" cannot answer simple questions concerning the use and purpose for the firearm, or the firearm does not seem suitable for the expressed purpose.
- While not a straw buy, others may resort to false identification or impersonation to thwart the system. Either way, both would require a person commit perjury to complete the sale, which is itself a crime.
- Purchasing several of the same firearm in a single sale.
- Multiple purchases made by the same buyer in a short period of time, such as one firearm a day over several days in a row.

None of these indicators are definitively suggestive of criminal activity and must be contemplated within the entire set of circumstances in a prospective sale situation, such as a persons buying several of the same firearm in a single sale. The buyer may be a collector of this specific type of firearm, or there could be a bonafide reason to buy several, such the stocking dealer having concurrently serial numbered guns, which certain buyers find desirable. On the other hand, in the author's experience, there were instances in which firearms were recovered literally days after the sale in which the possessor and the buyer were two different persons. In another incident, numerous firearms were recovered from a hotel room. There were several different persons who purchased the firearms and all the firearms had been purchased within weeks of the seizure. None of the purchasers of record was the actual possessor when the cache was uncovered.

## Theft

A prohibited person may just steal a firearm. If prohibited people know or believe they know where they can obtain a firearm by theft, this could be the most direct route to the ends. Family members, neighbors, friends, and associates known to possess firearms are often the first targets of these thefts. Would-be thieves often consider themselves above suspicion when they steal from someone close to them or may believe they could steal a firearm from someone who may not notice the firearm is missing for a period of time, maybe weeks or months. Even if confronted, the thief may attempt to manipulate the victim so the incident will not be reported. Whatever the circumstances, theft is theft, and it can occur from homes, vehicles, retailers, and common carriers as firearms are transported from place to place.

## Multi-Jurisdictional Co-Responsibility and Task Forces

Firearms are regulated by local, state, and federal laws woven into a complex patchwork of intersecting and overlapping jurisdictions. When multiple agencies have a stake in a matter, the key word to success is *cooperation*. If the operation is occurring within the scope of a task force, generally the lead agency that will actually carry the case has already been determined, and the efforts of the collective members of the task force are supporting the lead agency. However, absent this arrangement, coordination and cooperation between interested parties should be established and maintained, as it is in everyone's interest to do so. If an agency is offered participation in a task force, the author encourages the investment, which can only further advance the cause of public safety and give the agency a stake in participation to the focus of the task force. If an agency is approached with a proposal for a task force, the most competent and knowledgeable persons should be assigned to participate in order to obtain the maximum impact. Simply allocating a participant is not the most efficient and productive means of aiding the task force, especially if the person has no knowledge or competency in the matter at hand.

One particularly effective strategy is to pursue firearms and ammunition violations against prohibited persons. Often, and unfortunately, career criminals commit other crimes – murder, assaults, and robbery in particular – that are often difficult to build cases on due to lack of evidence and especially lack of witness cooperation. However, because such individuals are often involved in all types of criminal activity, if they can be apprehended in possession of firearms or ammunition, whether they are privately made firearms or not, this opens an avenue for prosecution that is easier to pursue. In such cases, the majority of witnesses are law enforcement personnel who are not deterred or intimidated into recanting their testimony. These cases do require a degree of physical evidence to successfully carry to fruition, but they have proven effective.

## Firearm Tracing

Much has been made about the inability to trace privately made firearms. Briefly, the ATF has an extensive investment in establishing and maintaining the capability enabling law enforcement agencies, both within and outside the United States, to trace firearms. Authorized users are able to submit trace requests, on an urgent basis if need be, and receive ATF trace data pertinent their trace request insomuch that they are willing to enter into a memorandum of understanding, especially as it pertains to further disclosures of trace data that the ATF provides.[3] In order to trace a firearm certain data from that firearm must be provided, among it the frame's serial number. Obviously, with a privately made receiver, there is no serial number recorded from which a trace could be started. There are two distinct exceptions: where state law or local ordinance requires registration of a privately made firearm, it is presumed those records could be accessed through the agency that is the custodian of records and used to determine the origin of the receiver. The second exception would be privately made regulated firearms, such as a suppressor. If such a privately made, regulated firearm were properly registered and payment of tax made, the firearm's existence is recorded by serial number. The reader is reminded that only a serial number present on the frame or receiver should be used as the identifying serial number, even if other numbers appear on other parts on the firearm such as a barrel or slide. A possible exception to this rule would be hybrid type craft guns which utilize gun parts coupled to crafted parts. A very atypical example shown in Figure 5.11, where it appears there are privately made Glock-style receivers which have been joined with original Glock manufactured slide to complete the firearm. In such a recovery, the slide serial number could potentially provide some value by tracing it, although this could be defined as a long shot at best. Since the slide is not a regulated component, it could have been separated from its original frame any time after the pistol was sold and changed hands any number of times without recordkeeping. Firearm tracing is certainly a valuable investigative tool; however, it is not the panacea that it is often heralded. The author has extensive experience tracing firearms and can attest to the value of the program; however, it does have limitations. Trace data may or may not offer much in the way of probative value in an investigation and may be more of an analytical tool in certain instances. When tracing firearms, there are certain caveats to bear in mind:

- Trace data might be incomplete due to age or poor record keeping.
- The firearm existed before record keeping requirements and has never passed through the hands of a licensee; therefore, there is no "paper" on this firearm.[4]
- Because firearms, particularly guns used in crimes, can change hands many times, the initial buyer or where the firearm was obtained may not be relevant.
- Misinterpretation or error in reporting firearm data results in erroneous information or trace results not being returned.
- If a firearm is reported stolen, the trace results are likely going to be moot; however, it could aid in corroborating an owner absent business records to substantiate the claim of ownership.
- A pattern of straw purchases or a single straw purchase are easily exposed using trace data as the initial indicator if the trace results are analyzed and a pattern is established.
- Although very infrequent, it is entirely possible that a crime-related firearm could be traced to its actual possessor when the possessor purchased the firearm, and it was subsequently alleged to have been used in a crime.

According to trace datum made public by the ATF (Calendar Year 2018 data), here is what traces tell us (see Figures 6.2–6.5).

What a firearm trace cannot determine is whether the firearm was actually used in a crime; only evidence can tell determine that. In any given crime – assault, battery, homicide, robbery, etc. – in which the firearm is used to facilitate the crime and is not recovered, there is no trace data from which to search upon. In other words, a firearm can only be traced if its identity is

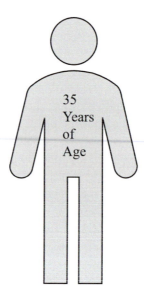

**Figure 6.2** 2018 Average age of possessor (ATF).

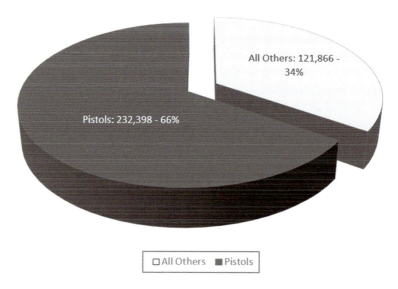

**Figure 6.3** In 2018, 336,549 firearms were traced. Of those, 215,180 were pistols.

known. The trace is made by serial number, so if there is no serial number, there can be no trace.[5] Therefore, without recovering a firearm and establishing its connection to a crime, any firearm is considered a "ghost gun" because nothing will be known about it absent any information that can be gleaned from the crime scene evidence. The firearm could have been a homemade

Investigative Considerations

**Figure 6.4** The average time to crime (TTC) for a firearm is 8.8 years after purchase.

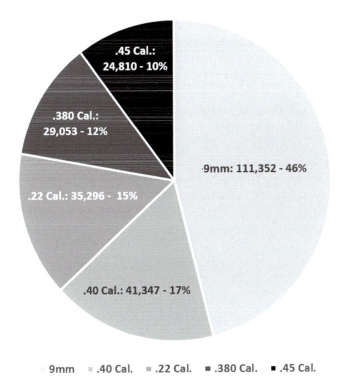

**Figure 6.5** Top calibers traced in 2018.

firearm, but it could be a firearm manufactured by a licensed entity just as easily, or it could have been legitimately purchased, a straw purchase, or stolen. Again, none of this is known, just postulated upon from the crime scene without having recovered a firearm and successfully establishing its relationship to the crime scene.

Consider this hypothetical situation. In 2018, ATF trace datum traced some 95,632 9mm firearms,[6] the most common caliber traced that year, in fact. According to the ATF, 2,099,319 9mm pistols were manufactured in 2018 alone,[7] let alone legacy firearms that may date back a century or more. If a 9mm firearm were used to commit a crime, and the firearm is not recovered, the tracing process is of no value. If the firearm is subsequently recovered, the trace does not necessarily reflect the name of the actor who committed the offense. If a suspect firearm is later recovered, it is entirely possible for comparative forensics to reveal the relationship between the recovered firearm and the crime scene, even if there is no direct connection established or known at the time of seizure. If the suspect firearm is determined to be homemade, this in no way diminishes the evidentiary value of the firearm and, in fact, may actually create additional lines of inquiry that could have the net effect of bolstering the case. As stated, trace data is valuable in certain investigative scenarios but of little value in others, and tracing the firearm is a matter of mere formalities.

The author is familiar with instances in which a firearm has been traced for investigative purposes absent the actual recovery of the firearm. The firearm was not in police custody when the trace request was filed, but the firearm's pedigree information was found from the factory shipping box and was used to file the trace request.

In spite of its limitations, do not discount firearms tracing, as it can provide substantial investigative information. For example, when a firearm is traced, the possessor's identity could be named in the trace submission, ensuring connections are made to this same individual should they be associated with future traces. Another possible investigative lead obtained from tracing is determining whether a certain firearm could have even existed at the time a crime is believed to have occurred. The author is familiar with at least one instance in which a lead was pursued using a firearm's serial number to determine not only who purchased the firearm but also when it was initially sold. The focus of the investigation was to determine whether a firearm could have been used by a suspect. As it turns out, the firearm in question did not even exist at the time the crime occurred. In this illustration, the trace results were valuable to explore a possible investigative lead, even if it did not pan out; however, the trace had to be assimilated with broader investigative information to be useful. Without a firm timeline on when the crime occurred, the trace data would provide little insight.

## Firearm Safety and Evidentiary Concerns

Under the most literal rules of evidence, exhibits are seized *in situ*, or "as-is"; however, this is not absolutely true. In an ideal world, evidence would not be even slightly altered, but this is simply not practical or realistic. The linear thinker could never untangle this concept in their minds; how could evidence be pristine, yet at the same time could there be bona fide reasons to alter the evidence? In fact, it is not uncommon for evidence to be altered from its original state in some way for perfectly legitimate purposes. Firearm seizures are a common example. Frequently, a loaded firearm is located under a car seat, hidden in a drawer, secreted inside a culvert after a shooting, concealed behind the padding in a baby car seat. Because of safety considerations, the firearm must be unloaded by removing the magazine (if a magazine fed firearm, opening the cylinder if a revolver), unloading the round from the chamber, and rendering it "safe" by locking or securing the action open. This, in fact, is a material alteration of the evidence, but it is overlooked, as it is a practical necessity because safety is the paramount concern with all other considerations secondary.

Evidence that is collected should somehow be documented, customarily through note taking, diagraming, surveys (measurements), and photographs. The extent and types of documentary measures taken are completely beholden to the whim of the collector and what is deemed appropriate and necessary in the investigative circumstances. Because firearms and related evidence are collected in any number of different physical locations under any number of circumstances, one is left with discretion and experience as the best guide because no one single path of documentation will be suitable for all situations. Collecting a firearm out of a typical automobile differs from taking it from a drawer within a private residence, lying in the open road, or from inside a culvert down the block from a shooting scene. Collectors of evidence, crime scene investigators, in particular, are reminded to avoid reliance on overly prescriptive routines and to use their best independent judgment during their scene-related activities; and searching is no exception. Searching is a manipulative process, and the searcher must have a keen eye and pay attention to avoid overlooking evidence.

## Investigative Circumstances

Investigations that involve homemade firearms are typically focused on three central themes:

- Clandestine manufacturing operations in which firearms are produced, assembled, and illicitly distributed.
- Homemade firearms seized in connection with a primary crime, such as homicide, robbery, assault, narcotics, or possession of a firearm by a prohibited person.
- Alerts, tips, or complaints made by third parties reporting suspicious activities, by information obtained from an informant, or anonymous reporter

In all instances, the paramount focus is on the safety of the investigative team. If the investigation has come to fruition, and there is going to be one or more search warrants executed, the scene must be secured by the entry team. An action plan should precede the execution of the warrant, and all participants in the warrant service should be present at the briefing, no matter their role. Once the warrant has been executed and the scene is secured, as expeditiously as possible, the location should be documented *in situ*. For example, in the case of a clandestine workshop, all tooling, projects, and raw materials should be depicted in state when the warrant was executed. Consider the following items for seizure:

- Firearm related matter – parts, accessories, devices in various stages of assembly, and receiver workpieces.
- Jigs, tooling, and machinery. If machinery is too cumbersome to seize, it should be extensively documented as to what type of machine tool it is so that its capabilities can be identified. If the machine tool is a CNC, consider attempting to record or copy its programming if it is used to mill receivers.
- Instructions, diagrams, machinist's drawings, and other like matter that is related to the fabrication and assembly of firearms.
- Mailings and packaging materials that are present on site, no matter where they are mailed from or to and regardless of recipient. The address labels can provide valuable information.
- Paper records – notebooks, ledgers, loose notes, and printouts reflecting transactions such as receipts substantiating the manufacturing activities on scene.
- Computers, laptops, and other electronic devices on site.
- Cell phones from any persons on scene with connection to the scene and/or the crime under investigation.
- Check the trashcans, dumpsters, and recycle bins for discarded residuals or aborted projects and builds.

## Encounters with Suspected Privately Made Firearms

If a firearm is seized, and the frame/receiver does not bear requisite identifying information, consider the following points:

- Know the law! Laws vary greatly state to state. **DO NOT PRESUME ANYTHING BASED UPON WHAT YOU INITIALLY SEE.**
- **DO NOT GUESS OR MISLEAD OTHERS BY INFERRING INTO MATTERS TO WHICH YOU ARE NOT COMPLETELY FAMILIAR!**

Investigative Considerations 113

- If this has occurred in a state or local venue that requires registration of a self-made firearm, determine its registration status, if any.
- Is the firearm. in its present configuration, a legal firearm? If there is uncertainty about the configuration or sum total of the parts, consulting with a competent firearm subject matter expert (SME) prior to proceeding with any formal action is **strongly recommended.**
- If sufficient legal grounds exist to seize the firearm, submit to evidence as you would any other firearm.
- Remember, privately made firearms may present specific safety concerns and may not be safe to fire. The firearm should not be disassembled or needlessly handled or manipulated except for the steps that are reasonably necessary to render the firearm safe for transport and storage.
- A credentialled and competent firearms SME should be consulted about the seizure. If the firearm is going to be evidence in a criminal case, the firearm must be subjected to routine examination.
- During any examinations, the firearm should be thoroughly photographed, and particular build features or unique properties noted for future reference.

## Potential Evidence

Although a privately made firearm may lack manufacturer information, this does not preclude the presence of potential physical evidence that could aid in many investigative circumstances. Figure 6.6 proposes one possible flow chart to extract the maximum amount of evidence.

- Fingerprints could possibly be obtained from the evidence and could affirm a person's contact with the firearm. If there is going to be a subsequent effort to collect DNA, sterile, single-use fingerprint supplies should be used.
- DNA collection may be appropriate in an effort to attach an individual to handling the firearm. The interior surfaces may prove more beneficial than the exterior because of subsequent handling and contamination. The builder, however, may have handled internal surfaces and components that otherwise are not further handled by the subsequent handlers. This could necessitate disassembling certain components to access deep crevices for DNA collection efforts. Do not overlook ammunition and magazines. Even fired casings have proven to be viable sources for identifiable DNA samples.
- Machinery or tools are used to cut receiver blanks. If the workshop is located, it may be possible to establish a relationship between a

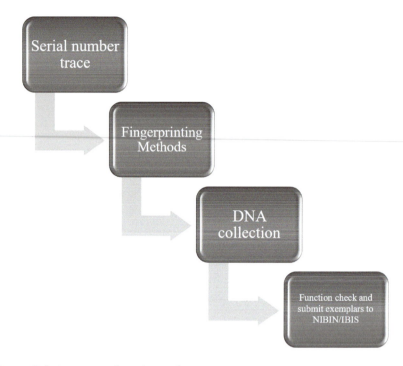

**Figure 6.6** A suggested evidence flow continuum.

receiver in evidence and tools used in its manufacture. Drill bits, end mills, and other cutting implements and tooling should be collected for potential toolmark comparisons with any suspect receivers.

## National Integrated Ballistics Information Network (NIBIN)

The NIBIN Program automates ballistics evaluations and provides actionable investigative leads in a timely manner. NIBIN is the only interstate automated ballistic imaging network in operation in the United States and is available to most major population centers in the United States.

Prior to the NIBIN Program, firearms examiners performed this process manually which was extremely labor intensive. To use NIBIN, firearms examiners or technicians enter cartridge casing evidence into the Integrated Ballistic Identification System. These images are correlated against the database. Law enforcement can search against evidence

# Investigative Considerations

from their jurisdiction, neighboring ones, and others across the country. This program is one investigative tool accessed by law enforcement that allows each of us to share information and cooperation easily making all of us more effective in closing cases.

(ATF, 2019)

The National Integrated Ballistics Information Network (NIBIN) has been in operation for approximately 20 years. There are distinct parallels in concept and application between NIBIN and AFIS (Automated Fingerprint Identification System). Imagery stored in NIBIN represents crime scene evidence or exemplars collected from known firearms test fired at the lab. The two sources are constantly cross-referenced looking for possible matches that could result in probative leads. To be clear, NIBIN does not make identifications; instead it suggests possible matches between entered exemplars. Figure 6.7 demonstrates NIBIN success, which, in effect, is a success story for all who have participated.

NIBIN relies on active participation and cooperation between NIBIN users to be successful. The more evidence that is captured and uploaded, the greater the library from which to reference. Agencies without direct NIBIN access should consider the investment and commitment to acquiring a workstation or, at the very least, ensuring seized firearms are transferred to an agency which will submit evidence examplars. NIBIN transcends time, physical distance, and continues working even when people are not. Evidence may have been seized, submitted years prior, and long forgotten by those who worked the case.

## Dealing with Persons

Investigators should make every effort to attempt to debrief persons apprehended with illegal homemade firearms.[8] Akin to the methods and techniques

**Figure 6.7** NIBIN success graphic (Infographic from the ATF).

used in many other styles of investigation, persons may be willing to provide information or assistance by cooperating with investigators through arrangements that demonstrate substantial assistance in the broader investigation in exchange for consideration in their own legal entanglement. Under the correct circumstances, an individual could be enlisted as a confidential informant.[9] The person conducting the debriefing should attempt to learn, at a minimum:

- How long the person has been in possession of the firearm.
- From whom and where was the firearm obtained?
- How did the person learn about the source and how did the person make a connection to the source?
- How much did the firearm cost?
- How does the supplier accept payment? What payment method/s are used?
- Is it possible to obtain additional firearms? If so, how?
- Is it possible to introduce undercover operatives to the source?
- Are there narcotics or other illegal activities concurrent to the access to guns?
- How does the person contact the source? Email, text, other messaging or social media platforms?

## Digital Forensics

In Chapter 1, the role and scope of the internet in homemade firearms was presented, and the role of technology has been recurrent throughout the text. If a clandestine manufacturing operation is uncovered, there is a strong likelihood that potential evidence resides on devices physically within or peripheral to the crime scene, including computers, portable storage media (portable hard drives, USB thumb drives, memory cards), smart phones, and tablets. Modern devices can be networked to anywhere from anywhere, and evidence may be contained in remote physical or virtual (cloud) environments. A CNC machine requires a program to operate, and this software suite may reside on a computer or smart device as an app, and there could be instructions for producing receivers or other gun parts in the library. The same applies to 3D printers. In either case, it may be necessary to utilize digital forensic SMEs to fully exploit the site. If available, these specialists could be brought to the warrant site to assist in seizing and collecting electronic evidence.

Portable electronic devices such as smart phones, tablets, and laptop computers should be placed inside a Faraday bag as quickly as possible.

Desktop type computers should be unplugged, not powered down by following on-screen prompts to shut down. In the case of on-site desktops or servers it may be advisable to bring digital forensic technicians in to collect such evidence.

Analysis of the devices seized could reveal internet browsing activities in which a person purchased precursor materials online, obtained guidance by watching or downloading videos and instructions, and communications related to building and selling firearms. It could be important to use the seized items and use the set up to create objects from the seized data libraries as demonstrative pieces or prove the ability to manufacture. This case evidence, even as demonstrative aids, substantiates the capability of the equipment to produce the items said to have been produced before being transferred to other parties.

## Coordination with Prosecutors

No matter how good the investigation appears, and no matter how much evidence is accumulated, the success of the case hinges on the ability of a prosecutor to either obtain a conviction through trial or successfully negotiate a plea arrangement, if appropriate. The investigators should take pride in their craft and be proud of their final work product, knowing that they have done the best that could possibly be done, even if not everything went to plan. Just because an arrest has been made does not relieve an investigator of any further responsibility to the case, as it now must be successfully prosecuted. In order to facilitate this, consider the following points:

- Attend and participate in pre-trial meetings.
- Ensuring reasonable evidence examinations are ordered and, when completed, results are disclosed in a timely manner.
- Accounting for all evidence as the trial date draws near. If evidence is off-site, arrangements should be made to have it returned in anticipation of trial.
- Actively play a role in devising a strategy to successfully prosecute the case.
- Familiarize the prosecutor with the more technical aspects of this type of investigation, perhaps even assisting in the formulating of questions to better aid the jury in understanding. It is very important that the prosecutor and witnesses, especially expert witnesses, have a good rapport between them.
- If investigators become aware of evidence or information that is exculpatory, they should notify the prosecuting attorney immediately.

- Be a good witness. Come prepared by reviewing case materials and appear professional in demeanor and attire. The witness must convey confidence and professionalism to even the most skeptical jury.

## Notes

1. A pretextual traffic stop is predicated on using an officer's observation of a traffic violation to stop a vehicle that is operating on the public roadway. The infraction is then used to enhance or further an investigation of the vehicle to include searching for contraband carried in the conveyance and determining if any of the occupants have outstanding warrants.
2. Case number 95-5841. Argued April 17, 1996 and decided June 10, 1996.
3. Portions of the disclosed datum is considered "tax" information and therefore its further dissemination is restricted.
4. Common, innocent examples include war souvenirs brought home by servicepersons, firearms that existed and were sold before record keeping requirements, and firearms that have never changed hands by a transaction that required any record be made.
5. Successful tracing can be hamstrung by obliterated, altered, or defaced serial numbers. Serial number restorative techniques are outside the purview of this text; however, a skilled examiner should be able to make a noble effort. Firearm tracing is also incumbent upon successfully entering the firearm's correct identifying information. Any person who traces firearms should be fluent with firearm marking practices and understand how to determine and locate the identifying information. This text emphasizes the critical importance of using only the frame affixed serial number as the proper identifier. Firearm tracing is yet another example of the author's stress on the point that only competent, skilled, and knowledgeable individuals should be involved in working with firearm evidence.
6. The trace data does not distinguish 9mm chambered pistols from rifles; therefore, for the purposes of this text, they are simply referred to as firearms.
7. 2018 ATF Annual Firearms Manufacturing and Export Report.
8. Or any case involving stolen or trafficked firearms.
9. Rule Number 1: never trust a confidential informant (CI). The reader is reminded that CIs have ulterior motives that seldom include a sense of civic duty or law and order.

## References

ATF. (2019, June 7). National Integrated Ballistic Information Network (NIBIN). Retrieved August 1, 2020, from *ATF official website*: https://www.atf.gov/firearms/national-integrated-ballistic-information-network-nibin

McHale, T. (2016, July 13). Buying and Selling a Firearm: Straw Purchases. Retrieved July 31, 2020, from *NRABlog*: https://www.nrablog.com/articles/2016/7/buying-and-selling-firearms-part-6-straw-purchases/

Mercer, M. (2020, September 3). Police 'Pretext' Traffic Stops Need to End, Some Lawmakers Say. Retrieved September 19, 2020, from *The Pew Charitable Trusts*: https://www.pewtrusts.org/en/research-and-analysis/blogs/stateline/2020/09/03/police-pretext-traffic-stops-need-to-end-some-lawmakers-say

Schneider, B. (2020, July 13). Berkeley Takes Cops Off Traffic Enforcement. Retrieved September 16, 2020, from *SFWeekly*: https://www.sfweekly.com/news/will-berkeley-take-cops-off-traffic-enforcement/

# Index

## A

Additive manufacturing, 63–64, 94, 95
    and 3D printing, 64–67
AFIS, see Automated Fingerprint Identification System
AK-47, 90
AK-type firearm, 90–91
*Anarchist's Cookbook*, 13
Anodizing, 80
"Any other weapon," 35–36, 44n29
AR-9, 79, 96n1
AR-10, 4, 21n5, 79
AR-15, 4, 21n5, 42n7, 79, 80
Armalite, 4, 21n4
Armalite Corporation, 4
Armalite pattern, 79–84
Armalite Rifle (AR), 4
Arms manufacturing, 2
AR-pattern upper receiver, 82
AR platform, 79, 80
AR receiver blank, 81
AR-type firearm, 79, 81
AR-type lower receiver, 69
Assault weapons, xiii
ATF's FTB, 9
Automated Fingerprint Identification System (AFIS), 115

## B

Barrel seat, 87
Braced handgun, 22n7
Brady Campaign to Prevent Gun Violence, 33, 34
Browning M1919-type firearm, 77n3
Build parties, 27
Bump stock, 44n26
Bureau of Alcohol, Tobacco, Firearms and Explosives (ATF), 9, 25, 32, 35, 42n9, 49, 51, 71

## C

Caliber, 22n11
Carbide 3D CNC machine, 74
Carbine, 21n2
Cast/forged receivers, 75
CI, see Confidential informant
Clandestine firearm manufacturing, 11
Class II drilling fixture, 69
Clip, 23n12
CNC, see Computerized Numerically Controlled machine
Cody Wilson Liberator pistol, 96
Colt .45, 85
Computerized Numerically Controlled (CNC) machine, 72–74, 77n4, 116
Confidential informant (CI), 100, 101
Controlled buys, 99–101
Controlled deliveries, 101–102
Coordination with prosecutors, 117–118
Craft/improvised suppressors, 93
Criminal enterprise, 19–20

## D

Dealing with persons, 115–116
Destructive device, 36–37
DEWAT, 55
Digital forensics, 116–117
Do-it-yourself (DIY) culture, 15–17
DOJ, see U.S. Department of Justice
Drop in auto sear (DIAS), 57

## E

80% receivers, 50, 72

## F

Firearm frame/receiver, 37, 47–51
    additive manufacturing and 3D printing, 63–67

CNC machinery, 72–74
components *vs.* accessories, 57
safety considerations, 54
tools, jigs, and fixtures, 67–72
Firearm safety and evidentiary concerns, 110–111
Firearm sales trends, 2020-2021, 31–32
Firearms Technology Branch (FTB), 9
Firearm suppressor, 38
Firearm tracing, 106–110
Firearm types and definitions, 35–40
Form 4, 4n31
Frangible ammunition projectiles, 75
FTB, *see* Firearms Technology Branch
Functional Kimber 8400 Magnum receiver, 26
Functional *vs.* operable firearm, 51–53

## G

GCA, *see* Gun Control Act
Ghost Gunner, 73
Ghost guns, xiii, xvii, 6–10, 42n8; *see also individual entries*
  role of technology in, 12–15
Glock, 4, 5
Glock factory, 88
Glock pattern handguns, 87–89
Glock-type GC9 blank, 9
Glock-type receiver, 88
Grandfathered status, 56
Guide Lamp Corporation, 91
Gun Control Act (GCA), xiii, xvi, 10, 29, 32, 49
Gun making, 1
  criminal enterprise, 19–20
  do-it-yourself (DIY) culture, 15–17
  ghost gun, 6–10
  ghost gun debate, technology role, 12–15
  improvised firearms, 10–12
  political motivations, 18
  prepper movement, 17–18
  privately made firearm, 19–20
  self-made gun movement, 5–6
  self-manufactured firearms, 20–21
Gunsmith fitting, 85
Gunsmithing, 17

## H

Hobbyist-level printers, 67
Homemade firearms, 97, 111

## I

IBIS/NIBIN, *see* Integrated Ballistic Identification System/National Integrated Ballistic Information Network
Improvised explosive devices (IEDs), 14
Improvised firearms, 10–12
Industrial Revolution, 1, 2
Integrated Ballistic Identification System/National Integrated Ballistic Information Network (IBIS/NIBIN), 53
International Traffic in Arms Regulations (ITAR), 15, 22n18
Investigative circumstances, 111–112
ITAR, *see* International Traffic in Arms Regulations

## J

Jigs, 67–69

## L

Large-format handgun, 5, 83
Liberator, 7, 91–92
  pistol design, 91
Licensed firearm manufacturers, growth trend, 30–31
Lightning Link, 57
Loopholes, 9
Lost and stolen firearms, 102–103

## M

M1911a1, 86
Machine gun, 37
Machine steel receivers, 74
Manufacture/manufacturing, 40
Maxim 50, 93
Metal injection molding, 75
Model 1911 and variants, 85–87
Mossberg 590 Nightstick, 6
Mossberg 930SPX pistol-grip shotgun, 40
Mossberg Shockwave, 5
Muffler/silencer, 37
Multi-jurisdictional co-responsibility and task forces, 105–106
Muzzleloader, 93

# Index

## N

National Firearms Act, 8, 22n15, 92
National Firearms Registration and Transfer Record (NFRTR), 41
National Instant Criminal Background System, 42n13
National Integrated Ballistics Information Network (NIBIN), 114–115
National Rifle Association (NRA), 44n26
NFRTR, *see* National Firearms Registration and Transfer Record
NIBIN, *see* National Integrated Ballistics Information Network
NICS, 43n15
1911A1 pistol
  left side of, 85
  right side of, 86
Non-guns, 54–56
Non-regulated components, 58–61
Non-regulated firearms manufacturing activity, 25–29
  opposition to, 32–34
Non-regulated parts, 58–59
NORINCO, 21n1
Nylon 66, 4

## O

OEM, *see* Original equipment manufacturer
Omega Firearms Suppressor, 14
Original equipment manufacturer (OEM), 89

## P

Parts kits, 76
PATs, *see* Power actuated tools
Pistol, 37
Pistol calibers, 80
Pistol-grip firearm, 39
Pistol stabilizing brace, 5, 83
Piston system, 80
Pivot pin, 82
PMF, *see* Privately made firearm
Polymer, 74–75
Polymer80, 50
Polymer-framed handguns, 74
Portable electronic devices, 116
Potential evidence, 113–114
Power actuated tools (PATs), 56

Prepper movement, 17–18
Prepping, 18
Pretextual traffic stop, 118n1
Privately made firearm (PMF), 19–20, 34, 42n2, 102
Prop, 56
Prototype Blackstar Arms rifle, 95
Public Safety and Recreational Firearms Use Protection Act, 21n6

## R

Rare Breed Triggers, 60
Receiver flats kits, 71
Regulated firearms manufacturing activity, 25–29
  in United States, 29–30
Remington Arms Company, 4
Remington modular combat shotgun, 36
Revolver, 38
Rifle, 39
Rock Island Armory, 23n21
Rock Island Arsenal – Joint Manufacturing and Technology Center (RIA-JMTC), 65, 66
Roh's machinery, 28
Ruger 10/22, 9, 89
Ruger AC-556, 38
Ruger AR-556 pistol, 6

## S

Self-made firearms
  encounters with, 112–113
  legalities affecting final configuration of, 34–35
  potential benefits of, 20–21
Self-made gun movement, 5–6
Self-made receiver, assembling and finishing, 75–77
Self-manufacturing, 16
  of regulated firearm, 40–41
Serial numbered parts, 61–62
Serial number restorative techniques, 118n5
Shotgun, 39
Shotgun barrel, 41
Side-plate receiver blanks, 71
SilencerCo, 93
Silencers, 14, 93
Single function of trigger, 37

Smith and Wesson Model 1917 revolver, 39
Solvent trap, 94
Stabilizing braces, 21n7
Standard fixed/collapsible style stocks, 83
STEN gun receiver, 70, 71
Straw sales, 104–105
Suppressors, 92–94
Survivalists, 18

## T

Theft, 105
.30 caliber and clip, 7
Thirty magazine clip, 7
Thompson/Center Arms Company, 35
3D-printed firearm, 19
3D printed Liberator parts, 91
Traffic stops, 98–99
Tubular receiver firearms, 92

## U

U.S. Army Ordnance Corps, 21n2
U.S. Army's Model 1873 Trapdoor Carbine, 2
U.S. Army's Rock Island Arsenal, 65
U.S. Department of Justice (DOJ), 27

## V

Vickers-/Maxim-type machine gun, 72, 77n3
Vintage parts kits, 78n5
Violent Crime Control and Law Enforcement Act of 1994, 21n6
VP-70, 75

## W

Walther PP frame, 48
Weapon made from rifle, 39
Weapon made from shotgun, 39
Weapons parts kit, 51
Winchester Repeating Arms, 21n3

## Z

Zamak, 75
Zip guns, 10, 11